T0351147

Mastering Visual Studio Code

Mastering Visual Studio Code empowers the readers to get the most out of VS Code, an extremely popular and powerful code editor.

Microsoft's Visual Studio Code (VS Code) is a free and open-source code and text editor. Despite its modest size, VS Code includes numerous significant features that have made it one of the most popular code editors in recent years.

VS Code is compatible with various programming languages, including Java, C++, Python, CSS, Go, and Docker files. VS Code also lets you add and create new extensions, such as code linkers, debuggers, and support for cloud and web development. Compared to other text editors, the VS Code user interface allows for a lot of interactivity.

Some of the major advantages of Visual Studio Code are:

- Cross-stack development using an open technology platform

- Huge repository of plug-ins produced by the community and professionals

- Debug tools for generic usage

- Cross-platform support, including Linux, Mac, and Windows

A good and powerful code editor is a vital part of any developer's toolkit. VS Code has all the features any developer might need. As such, learning Visual Studio Code and understanding its various offerings and features is a good idea.

With *Mastering Visual Studio Code*, using VS Code will become a breeze, regardless of the language that you are coding in, thereby boosting your productivity.

The *Mastering Computer Science* series is edited by Sufyan bin Uzayr, a writer and educator with more than a decade of experience in the computing field.

Mastering Computer Science
Series Editor: Sufyan bin Uzayr

Mastering Visual Studio Code: A Beginner's Guide
Jaskiran Kaur, D Nikitenko, and Mathew Rooney

Mastering Django: A Beginner's Guide
Jaskiran Kaur, NT Ozman, and Reza Nafim

Mastering Ubuntu: A Beginner's Guide
Jaskiran Kaur, Rubina Salafey, and Shahryar Raz

Mastering KDE: A Beginner's Guide
Jaskiran Kaur, Mathew Rooney, and Shahryar Raz

Mastering Kotlin: A Beginner's Guide
Divya Sachdeva, Faruq KC, and Aruqqa Khateib

Mastering Rust: A Beginner's Guide
Divya Sachdeva, Faruq KC, and Aruqqa Khateib

For more information about this series, please visit: https://www.routledge.com/Mastering-Computer-Science/book-series/MCS

The "Mastering Computer Science" series of books are authored by the Zeba Academy team members, led by Sufyan bin Uzayr.

Zeba Academy is an EdTech venture that develops courses and content for learners primarily in STEM fields, and offers education consulting to Universities and Institutions worldwide. For more info, please visit https://zeba.academy

Mastering Visual Studio Code

A Beginner's Guide

Edited by Sufyan bin Uzayr

CRC Press
Taylor & Francis Group
Boca Raton London New York

CRC Press is an imprint of the
Taylor & Francis Group, an **informa** business

First edition published 2023
by CRC Press
6000 Broken Sound Parkway NW, Suite 300, Boca Raton, FL 33487-2742

and by CRC Press
4 Park Square, Milton Park, Abingdon, Oxon, OX14 4RN

CRC Press is an imprint of Taylor & Francis Group, LLC

© 2023 Sufyan bin Uzayr

Library of Congress Cataloging-in-Publication Data

Names: Bin Uzayr, Sufyan, editor.
Title: Mastering Visual studio code : a beginner's guide / edited by Sufyan bin Uzayr.
Description: First edition. | Boca Raton : CRC Press, 2023. | Series: Mastering computer science series | Includes bibliographical references and index.
Identifiers: LCCN 2022020958 (print) | LCCN 2022020959 (ebook) | ISBN 9781032319063 (hardback) | ISBN 9781032319056 (paperback) | ISBN 9781003311973 (ebook)
Subjects: LCSH: Microsoft Visual studio. | Web site development--Computer programs. | Application software--Development.
Classification: LCC TK5105.8885.M57 M19378 2023 (print) | LCC TK5105.8885.M57 (ebook) | DDC 006.7/882--dc23/eng/20220819
LC record available at https://lccn.loc.gov/2022020958
LC ebook record available at https://lccn.loc.gov/2022020959

ISBN: 9781032319063 (hbk)
ISBN: 9781032319056 (pbk)
ISBN: 9781003311973 (ebk)

DOI: 10.1201/9781003311973

Typeset in Minion
by Deanta Global Publishing Services, Chennai, India

Contents

Mastering Computer Science Series Preface

T HE *Mastering Computer Science* series covers a wide range of topics, spanning programming languages as well as modern-day technologies and frameworks. The series has a special focus on beginner-level content, and is presented in an easy to understand manner, comprising:

- Crystal-clear text, spanning various topics sorted by relevance

- Special focus on practical exercises, with numerous code samples and programs

- A guided approach to programming, with step-by-step tutorials for the absolute beginners

- Keen emphasis on real-world utility of skills, thereby cutting out the redundant and seldom-used concepts and focusing instead on industry-prevalent coding paradigm

- A wide range of references and resources, to help both beginner- and intermediate-level developers gain the most out of the books

The *Mastering Computer Science* series of books start from the core concepts, and then quickly move on to industry-standard coding practices, to help learners gain efficient and crucial skills in as little time as possible. The books assume no prior knowledge of coding, so even the absolute newbie coders can benefit from this series.

The *Mastering Computer Science* series is edited by Sufyan bin Uzayr, a writer and educator with more than a decade of experience in the computing field.

About the Editor

Sufyan bin Uzayr is a writer, coder, and entrepreneur with more than a decade of experience in the industry. He has authored several books in the past, pertaining to a wide variety of topics, ranging from history to computers/IT.

Sufyan is the Director of Parakozm, a multinational IT company specializing in EdTech solutions. He also runs Zeba Academy, an online learning and teaching vertical with a focus on STEM fields.

Sufyan specializes in a wide variety of technologies, such as JavaScript, Dart, WordPress, Drupal, Linux, and Python. He holds multiple degrees, including ones in management, IT, literature, and political science.

Sufyan is a digital nomad, dividing his time between four countries. He has lived and taught in universities and educational institutions around the globe. Sufyan takes a keen interest in technology, politics, literature, history, and sports, and in his spare time enjoys teaching coding and English to young students.

Learn more at sufyanism.com.

CHAPTER 1

Introduction to VS Code

IN THIS CHAPTER

➤ Introduction to Visual Studio Code

➤ Visual Studio vs. Visual Studio Code

➤ Pros and cons

➤ Features

In this chapter, we will be learning some basic aspects of VS Code like its installation, use, interface, built-in extensions, and third-party package installation.

So, VS Code stands for Visual Studio Code. It is the first code editor and cross-platform development tool source-code editor made for various popular operating systems, i.e., Microsoft, Windows, Linux, and macOS. It includes various features like debugging, syntax, intelligent code completion, snippets code, refactoring, auto-indentations, brackets matching, highlighting, support for dozens of languages, fast code editor day by day, and embedded Git. Users can change their coding themes and keyboard shortcuts and install extensions, preferences, and other fantastic functionality.

VS Code was announced for the first time on April 29, 2015, at a 2015 Microsoft conference. It was organized at the Moscone Center in San Francisco from April 20 to May 1, 2015. Then on November 18, 2015, the natural source of VS Code was released under an MIT license and made available on GitHub. MIT license I permits the reuse of code

DOI: 10.1201/9781003311973-1

for any purpose. Suppose an organization has an original MIT license; in that case, they can make any kind of changes to their own needs. GitHub is a web-based interface that uses Git (Global Information Tracker). It keeps track of the changes you make to files so that you have a record of what you (or others) have done to your files. The open-source version control software lets several changes be made to various pages at the same time.

It provides programmers with a new choice of developing tools that combine the simplicity of a code editor and with a smooth-running experience to meet developers' needs for core coding. For serious coding, the developer frequently needs to work with code. This code editor includes built-in support for always-on IntelliSense code completion, rich code semantics, understanding and navigation, and code refactoring. The editor code contains built-in support for Node.js development with TypeScript and JavaScript, ASP.NET Core development with C#, C++, Python, PHP, Go, and runtimes such as Unity and .NET. It also works with web technologies such as HTML, CSS, Sass, Less, and JSON. Its code integrates with packages and repositories. VS Code understands Git and delivers excellent Git workflows. It can combine various languages such as Node. js and JavaScript for the speed and flexibility of native apps. Debugging is the most popular feature in Visual Code Editor. The entire environment of this editor can become flexible through the use of extensions. It is always up to date.

WHEN AND WHY TO USE VISUAL STUDIO CODE

Before you start learning how to use Visual Studio Code, what features it offers, and how it provides an improved coding experience, you need to understand its motive clearly. Visual Studio Code is not just a simple code-based editor; it is a robust environment that has writing code at its core. The main point of Visual Studio Code is to make coding for web development, mobile development, and cloud development platforms easier for any developers working on various operating systems like Linux, Windows, and macOS, making you independent from proprietary development environments.

To combine all these features into a tool, Visual Studio Code provides a coding environment based on folders, making it easy to work with code files that are not organized within projects and offering a unified way to work with different languages. Starting from this assumption, code offers an advanced editing experience with features common to any supported languages, plus some features available to specific languages. As you will learn throughout this book, code also makes it easy to extend its built-in features by supplying custom languages, syntax coloring, editing tools, debuggers, and more via several extensibility points. It is a code-centric tool with a primary focus on web and cross-platform code. That said, it does not provide all of the features you need for complete, more complex application development and application lifecycle management. It is not intended to be used with some development platforms.

Visual Studio Code can be installed on Windows 7, 8, and 10. For the Windows operating system, Visual Studio Code is available with two installers:

1. A global installer

2. A user-level installer

The global installer requires administrative privileges for installation. The user-level installer makes code available only to the logged user, but it does not require administrative rights.

INSTALLATION OF VISUAL STUDIO CODE ON MACOS

Installing VS Code on macOS is very simple. From the VS Code download page, click the "Download for macOS" button and wait for the download to complete. On macOS, Visual Studio Code works as an individual program, and therefore you need to double-click the downloaded file to start the application.

INSTALLING VISUAL STUDIO CODE ON LINUX

Linux is a popular operating system, and many derived distributions exist, so there are different installers available depending on the distribution you are using. For the Ubuntu and Debian distributions, you will need the .deb installer. For the Red Hat Linux, Fedora, and SUSE distributions, you will need the .rpm installer. This clarification is necessary because, unlike Windows and macOS, the browser might not detect the Linux distribution you are using automatically, and therefore it will offer both options. Once installed, you simply need to click the "Show Applications" button on the desktop and then the Visual Studio Code shortcut.

DIFFERENCE BETWEEN THE TEXT EDITOR AND THE IDE (INTEGRATED DEVELOPMENT ENVIRONMENT)

The words "text editor" and "IDE" are generally used to write the code pleasantly and cleanly. They enhance the productivity of programming code and allow the user to perform various actions in their code.

As a web developer, you should be aware of the difference between "text editor" and IDE (Integrated development environment).

WHAT IS CODE EDITOR?

There are various popular coding editors these days. Developers and programmers use these to manipulate plain text source code, configure files or documentation, or view error logs. A text editor has a more comprehensive approach than an IDE because, with the help of it, we can code using different languages. It is one step down from the full functionality of an integrated development environment. Text editors are fast and light and allow for efficient programming. They provide features like regular expression search, replace, syntax highlighting, auto-completion, search, multi-tabs, and panes. An IDE is too restrictive because you first need to learn about the IDE environment. It isn't enjoyable to make things understandable because it doesn't automatically help you complete them. If you want to do a simple project in IDE, it might annoy you that first you have to understand the project's structure.

Some commonly used text editor software:

- Visual Studio Code

- Notepad++

- Sublime Text

- Atom

- Brackets

- Ultra Edit

- Text Edit

- G Edit

- EditPlus

- BB Edit

- Text Mate

WHY DO WE NEED A TEXT EDITOR?

If you work on a project, you will not save your whole project in an online editor like Codecademy, Scratchpad, io, js fiddle, and JSBin when you make your online project edits. It is also impossible to edit your code in Microsoft Word pages, Google Docs, or Office.

WHAT CAN A TEXT EDITOR DO?

It is acceptable to use Notepad in the beginning just by writing the file extension; for example, for HTML the file extension would be .html; for CSS (Cascading style sheet) the file extension would be .css; for Python the file extension would be .py; and soon you can go with this criteria. Choosing the best code editor makes your work easy and handy. Some good things text editors can do:

- Tell you where there is an error within your code

- Create multiple files and folders

- Perform multi-tasks like creating and opening files at once

- Delete various folders and files once

- Highlight syntax (display multiple types of code in different colors)

WHAT IS A RICH TEXT EDITOR?

It is a text toolbar that has an icon for editing and formatting your text. You can use the text editor to include links, images, audio, and text, and it can also create a blog, note section, comment section, and more.

An example of a Rich Text Editor Toolbar is shown in Figure 1.1.

WHAT ARE IDES?

Turbo Pascal launched the idea of an IDE, but many believe that Microsoft's Visual Basic (VB) was established in 1991.

Benefits of IDEs

IDEs work to improve developer productivity and time. These IDEs boost the speed of tasks, keeping developers up to date with best practice.

FIGURE 1.1   Editor toolbar.

- **Faster development tasks:** IDEs have tighter integration tasks means boosted productivity. For example, the developers can parse code and check syntax while editing, allowing instant syntax for errors. In addition, the tools and features of the IDE help programmers organize, prevent, and implement shortcuts.

- **Up to date:** It can stay up to date with new features. A developer who wants to learn constantly and stay up to date is more like to add value to the team and the organization, boosting productivity.

- **Standardization:** It regulates the development, helps programmers work together, and assists new hires.

Languages Supported by IDEs

Multiple-language IDEs, like Eclipse (C, C++, Java, Python, Perl, PHP, and many more), Komodo (Perl, C, C++, Perl, and more) and Net Beans (Java, PHP, Ruby, C, C++, and more) exist. Developers can use any IDE for their languages. There are various multi-language IDEs, such as:

- **Eclipse:** It supports C, C++, Python, Perl, PHP, JAVA, and many others. It is a free and also open-source editor for various development frameworks. It began for the Java development environment. It has expanded through plug-ins. This IDE is managed and directed by Eclipse.org.

- **Komodo IDE:** Supports Perl, Python, TCL, JavaScript, and more. It is an enterprise-level tool with a more expensive price point.

- **Net Beans:** It supports Java, JavaScript, C, C++, Ruby, and more. Modules provide all functions of the IDE. It is free and open-source.

- **Aptana:** It supports HTML, JavaScript, CSS, AJAX, and others through plug-ins. It is a popular choice for web-based development.

- **Geany:** It supports C, PHP, Java, HTML, Perl, Pascal, and many more.

IDE SPECIFIC TO APPLE OR MICROSOFT

The following IDEs are specific to Apple or Microsoft:

- **Visual Studio:** It supports VB.NET, Visual C++, C#, F#, and more. It is Microsoft's IDE, designed to create apps for the platform.

- **MonoDevelop:** It supports the Visual basic, C/C++, C#, and additional .NET languages.

- **Xcode:** It supports Swift and Objective-C language, as well as Cocoa and Cocoa touch APIS. This IDE is solely for creating iOS and Mac applications.

- **Espresso:** It supports the XML, HTML, CSS, PHP, and JavaScript. It is a tool for Mac web programmers.

- **Coda:** It supports PHP, HTML, CSS, AppleScript, and Cocoa API.

IDE	Text Editor
It is a full-fledged software environment that consolidates essential developer tools and is required to build and test software.	A text editor is just simply a computer program and tools used for editing and plain text.
IDEs have different aspects of a computer program into a single graphical user interface.	A text editor simply takes some input, changes it, and produces some output.
IDEs require more disk space, more memory, and speed.	A text editor requires fewer hardware resources to run, resulting in more disk space memory and processing power.
IDE may cost around $70 or so, while high-end IDEs can easily cost hundreds of dollars.	A simple text editor may cost around $20, while a professional full functional text editor can cost you about $100.
Eclipse and IntelliJ are IDEs built for Java, and Xcode is an IDE designed for the Apple platform. Some well-known examples of IDEs are Eclipse, IntelliJ IDES, Visual Studio, Code Block, NetBeans, and many more.	Standard text editors include Notepad, Sublime, Text Mate, Brackets, and so on.
Key features include text, editing, compiling, debugging, GUI, syntax, highlighting, unit testing, and more.	Key features include syntax, highlighting, printing, multi-view, and preview windows.

VARIOUS IDS COMPARISON

What is MonoDevelop's IDE?

It is accessible to the general public for the development of web and desktop-based applications. It runs on macOS, Windows, and Linus systems and allows the user to only focus on Mono. It does not allow many formatting features.

KEY DIFFERENCES BETWEEN MONODEVELOP AND VISUAL STUDIO

MonoDevelop IDE does not provide you with the facility to style the code. In contrast, there are many options available in Visual Studio for code styling according to the development requirements.

MonoDevelop is a cross-platform IDE, whereas Visual Studio can be considered a suite with all the tools required for the development.

There are many more performance issues in the Visual Studio. It is pretty large and uses a lot of necessary resources while running even a remote code, while MonoDevelop is lighter and runs code very quickly.

Due to having so many drawbacks and a lack of features, many people still use MonoDevelop.

Major differences between MonoDevelop and Visual Studio are shown below.

MonoDevelop	Visual Studio
It is a cross-platform IDE for C#, F#, and so on, which allows developers to write web- and desktop-based applications on Linus, Unix, Mac, etc.	It is united by having component-based software development tool building applications for devices, cloud, etc.
It is comparatively faster, lighter, so it consumes less power and resources. So applications run faster on it.	It is slower and larger than MonoDevelop and also uses fewer resources while running any application.
MonoDevelop is a lightweight IDE, i.e., it can also run on any system even with fewer configurations.	It is a very large IDE and requires more than 12GB of space to run smoothly on any system, which makes it an issue for developers.
It is less stable compared to Visual Studio.	It is more stable and can deal with all types of projects, whether small or large.
No plug-ins are provided to the programmer or developer in MonoDevelop IDE.	Visual Studio provides the advantage of installing various paid as well as free plug-ins.
There is less community support for the MonoDevelop IDE.	People globally prefer Visual Studio more as their IDE to develop core code. It has a large community in comparison to MonoDevelop.
Some of the tools that integrate with MonoDevelop are C#. Asp.NET, MySQL SQLite, etc.	Some of the tools that integrate with VS are Windows, Azure Function, etc.
Some of the essential features provided by MonoDevelop IDE are automatic code completion, GUI, source control, etc.	Some of the essential features provided by Visual Studio are tools available for editing, code class designer, database schema, etc.

HISTORY OF VS

Its first version was introduced on December 4, 1997; its code name is Boston version 5.0 with service pack 3. It was written in Java, HTML, JavaScript, CSS, and TypeScript. It was sold as a bundle with the separate IDEs used for Visual C++, Visual Basic, and Visual FoxPro.

WHAT IS VS (VISUAL STUDIO)?

Microsoft Visual Studio is an IDE made by Microsoft and is used for different types of software development such as websites, web apps, web services, mobiles, and so on. It contains completion tools, compilers, and other features to facilitate the software development process. It includes code editor support like IntelliSense as well as code refactoring.

It works as a source-level debugger and a machine-level debugger. It includes a code profiler, GUI application, web designer, and database schema designer. It supports a total of 36 different programming languages and allows the code editor debugger to use them. Most editions of Visual Studio, including the Community edition, are available free of charge. It helps you to build any applications and games using supported languages. It is for ensuring that once the application is deployed, it will run smoothly as tested. Microsoft IDE is produced by a community of C# and .NET developers. It can build and maintain .NET through a selection of Azure plug-ins. It is available for Windows and macOS users.

Features of VS

1. Build environment and output

2. Test development

3. Debugging tools and break points

4. And much more

Features of IDE

1. Visual Studio Team Services

2. Power BI Pro

3. SQL

4. Exchange

5. Azure Developer Services

6. SharePoint

7. Office 365 Developer

Benefits

The main advantages of VS IDEs are as follows:

1. **Coding assistance:** It supports real-time coding assistance with its built-in IntelliSense, which provides descriptions. Also, Visual Assist is a plug-in for Microsoft Visual Studio. It primarily enhances code suggestions and provides IntelliSense and syntax highlighting.

2. **Collaboration support:** This platform is equipped with collaborative capabilities just for increasing the productivity of the team. Live sharing is an extension that enables real-time collaboration between developers. You can share your session with someone else, allow them to edit and update, as well as share a server session.

3. **High customizability:** One of the most extending functionalities of IDE is by using add-ons and extensions. The developer, too, can publish their very own extensions or add-ons.

4. **Testing platform:** It has a host of tools, which are available in all of the languages for easing debugging. The debugging can be done remotely, locally, or even in the middle of the deployment.

Some commonly used text editor Software:

1. Visual Studio Community

2. Visual Studio 2019

3. Visual Studio 2017

4. JBuilder

5. XCode

6. Eclipse

7. Net beans

8. Android Studio

IS VISUAL STUDIO FREE?

The primary community edition is free; it is a fullly featured, extensible, and free IDE to create modern applications for Android, Windows, IOS, Windows, and application and cloud services. It is for students, open-source, and individual developers. It is one of the most admired IDEs out there. It has a large community and also supports individual developers and small teams.

Make sure your PC is ready for Visual Studio.

Before installing Visual Studio

1. Check the system requirements. You should have a 64-bit operating system. The Visual Studio is not made for 32-bit and ARM operating systems.

2. Apply the latest Windows updates. Make sure that your operating system has the newest security and required system components for VS.

3. The reboots of your system ensure that any pending installs or updates do not create any problem for your Visual Studio install.

Download Visual Studio

Visit Visual Studio's official site to download the latest version as per your needs; now install the Visual Studio Installer.

1. vs_community.exe for Visual Studio Community

2. vs_professional.exe for Visual Studio Professional

3. vs_enterprise.exe for Visual Enterprise Professional

Click Continue to begin the setup installation of Visual Studio.

Then choose workloads, as per your need; its workload consists of ASP. NET and web development, Azure development, Python development, Node development, and more for desktop and mobile. Then start the installation.

Choose your components; you can add more components than work-loads. Choose your language pack to select your installation location manually if you want to after completing the installation.

Now you can start developing.

VISUAL STUDIO INSTALLATION IN WINDOWS

Installation

1. Download the Visual Studio Code installer for Windows.

2. Once it is downloaded, run the installer setup.

3. By default, VS Code is installed.

What Is Visual Studio Code?

It is a free, open-source text editor developed by Microsoft. VS Code is available for all the operating systems such as Windows, Linux, and macOS. This editor is relatively lightweight, and it includes some powerful features that have made the VS Code the most popular development environment.

VS Code supports a wide range of programming languages from Python to CSS, Go, and Dockerfiles; it allows you to include code linkers, debuggers, and cloud web development support. VS Code is built on Node .js Electron (JavaScript Framework), HTML, and CSS.

To simplify the user experience, VS Code is divided into five regions:

1. The activity bar

2. The sidebar

3. Editor groups

4. The panel

5. The status bar

There are various features listed below:

- **Status bar:** User can see their program errors and warnings from the status bat. Its shortcut is Ctrl + Shift + M.

- Split View

- **Zen mode:** It is used to hide all the UI except the editor like no Activity bar, Status bar, Side Bar and Panel) move to the entire screen. It can be toggled using the View menu or by the shortcut Ctrl + K Z.

- Command Line

- **Git integration:** It will come with the Git integration that allows you to commit, pull, and push your code changes to a remote Git repository.

- **Command Palette:** By pressing the Ctrl + Shift + P keys, it brings up the Command Palette, from where you can access all the functionality of VS Code.

- **Default keyboard shortcuts:** If you forget the keyboard shortcut, you can use the Command Palette to help yourself. All of the commands are present in the Command Palette.

- Change language mode

- **Git support:** Your project resources can be pulled from Git Hub Repo online, and saving can be done too.

- **Commenting:** A standard feature but some of the programming languages do not support this commenting. It helps you to track all the work.

Visual Studio scope

The most common programming supported by VS Code is:

- C#
- GO
- JavaScript
- R
- XML
- JSON
- PERL
- CSS
- SASS
- LESS

Advantages of Visual Studio Code

It helps you to develop web apps for customers' needs.

It has a good navigation features, better search and filters, and previews the code.

Visual Studio Code will help you to create native apps for Android, iOS, and Windows.

If you are working on Angular or Angular and React for UI, VS is the best way to support TypeScript and Javascript.

Disadvantages of Visual Studio Code

Its installation and updation may take time.

Sometimes VS Code needs extensive research to solve differences within projects.

COMPARISON TABLE: VISUAL STUDIO VS VISUAL STUDIO CODE

Visual Studio	Visual Studio Code
It is an IDE.	It is a text code editor where you can edit every coding file.
It is a slow cross-platform as it processes slower than a text editor.	It is faster compared to Visual Studio.
It uses more of the CPU, which leads to a slower system.	It is lightweight, which makes it faster.
Aside from the free text editor, Visual Studio has a paid version IDE as well.	It is a free and open-source text editor.
It uses the best and most advanced IntelliSense.	Visual Studio Code has the latest version of IntelliSense.
It requires ample space to work on and install.	It does not need a large download size, the same as Visual Studio.
It is used for compiling the code of different languages.	It can't be used for compiling the code of different languages.
It allows for working on multiple windows.	It doesn't allow for working on multiple windows.
The user might face various difficulties with their setup and setting of Visual Studio.	It is very straightforward to set up and use as compared to VS.
It supports .NET, C/C++ (windows), C# projects along with the database, SQL, and so on.	It supports HTML/JavaScript files.

(Continued)

Visual Studio	Visual Studio Code
Companies using Visual Studio:	Companies using Visual Studio Code:
Accenture	HENCE
Alibaba Group	CRED
Microsoft	Freetrade
Via Vare	Alibaba group
joIntuit	Deleo
Integrated Tools:	Integrated Tools:
.Net core	GitHub.Net Core
Azure DevOps	Windows
Windows	Azure Functions
Azure Function	TS
Sauce Labs	Lint
Price:	Price:
Community (Free)	Free
Business ($45/month)	
Enterprise ($250/month)	

VISUAL STUDIO VS VISUAL STUDIO CODE
Features Differences

Visual Studio	Visual Studio Code
Code editor: Like the other IDEs, Visual Studio involves a code editor, which is helpful for code completion and syntax highlighting with the help of IntelliSense used for functions, loops variable, methods, and LINQ queries. Additionally, it supports the bookmark setting within the core code which helps with quick navigation.	Language support: Visual Studio Code supports brackets matching, syntax highlighting, code floating, and configurable snippets. It also works with IntelliSense for languages like TypeScript, CSS, JavaScript, JSON, and HTML. It provides debugging support to Node.js.
Debugger: It allows some breakpoint settings (which means you can stop execution wherever you want) and watches (to match the variable's value). The debugger supports Continue & Edit, which means if you put a mouse pointer to an instance, it will display the current value in a tooltip, and then you can easily modify it.	Data collection: Its main functions are to collect information and transfer it to Microsoft. All the organized codes are freely available to the public as it is also an open-source application.

(Continued)

Visual Studio	Visual Studio Code
Designer: Various designing tools help the user in the development of the application, and the tools are:	Version control: It has dedicated tabs in the main menu bar to access various studio version controls settings to check the changes made in the current project. It allows users to make repositories and also gives a pull, including push requests directly from the programs.
1. Windows Forms Designer: It is used for developing graphical user interface applications. 2. WPF Designer: It creates XAML code for the UI. 3. Web development/designer: It is used for ASP.NET applications. 4. Data designer: It can design by analyzing the graphical view. 5. Class designer: It is used for creating class diagrams. 6. Mapping designer: It is used for design mapping classes and database schemas.	
It includes several tools to create dependent graphs.	VS Code has an individual integrated terminal.
It has WYSIWYG editors for C++, .NET, .VB. NET, and C#.	To increase the efficiency of the Visual Studio Code, users need to install extra packages.

WHAT IS INTELLISENSE?

It is a general term for various code editing features, including code completion and parameters member lists. It is provided for JavaScript, JSON, HTML, and CSS out of the box. You can enable the IntelliSense feature by typing trigger characters (such as the dot (.) character) in JavaScript.

WHICH ONE IS BEST: VISUAL STUDIO OR VISUAL STUDIO CODE?

Deciding which one is best is not an easy task. Suppose your development method is test-driven, Visual Studio will be the best. On the other hand, in Visual Studio Code, there are 15 test-driven extensions for development supporting Node.js, Go, PHP, and. NET.

Although Visual Studio does a brilliant job working with databases, mainly Microsoft SQL Server and its relatives, Visual Studio Code has a lot of database extensions.

Visual Studio does not work on Linux, but Visual Studio Code does.

If you work on development project for hours, then Visual Studio is better than Visual Studio Code. Visual Studio Code might be good for you if you code for short periods and switch between other tasks.

ATOM VS VISUAL STUDIO CODE

What Is Atom?

It is a free and open-source text editor developed by GitHub itself. It works across Windows, macOS, and Linux. It is currently at version 1.52.0. It lets you easily customize every aspect of it to speed up your workflows. It uses a framework called Electron. Electron is a JavaScript framework that enables the building of multi-platform desktop applications. It is built with web technologies such as HTML, CSS, and JavaScript, making it more flexible and hackable. If you know these technologies, extending them is very easy. There are over 50,000 packages and over 3000 themes. It can help you to create an interactive and responsive web application.

	Atom	Visual Studio Code
Initial release date	February 26, 2014	April 19, 2015
Developers	GitHub	Microsoft
Supported	Windows/Linux/macOS	Windows/Linux/macOS
License by	MIT License	MIT License
Extension support	Yes	Yes
Cross-platform	Yes	Yes
Syntax highlighting	Yes	Yes
Auto-completion	Yes	Yes
Inbuilt version control	Yes	Yes
Multiple selection editing	Yes	Yes
Price	Free	Free

Features of Atom vs VS Code

1. **Configuration:** Configuration in VS Code involved using JSON files before, but now graphical user interface (GUI) replaces that. It is simple to use a GUI, and it works well.

   In Atom, you have GUI all around to edit instead of having a JSON file to edit. Users can report if they are facing issues during the configuration process.

2. **Customization and extensibility:** Both are extensible and customizable with other third-party add-on packages. Both editors allow you to search, install, and manage the extensions directly inside the program.

3. **Plug-ins and integrations:** In the VS Code, plug-ins add more features and functionality to the program. It also includes language support, themes, commands, Git integration, debuggers, and more.

   Atom gives more power and functionality to various plug-ins. It has many built-in and third-party plug-ins.

4. **Git integrations:** VS Code has built-in Git integrations and many GitHub-related extensions, whereas Atom is a product of GitHub and has Git integration as a built-in feature.

   Atom, Git integration is provided by navigating to View > Toggle Git Tab/Toggle GitHub Tag.

   In Visual Studio Code, Git integration is provided through the GitHub Pull Request and Issues extension.

5. **Auto-completion:** This tool lets you view and insert possible completions in the editor. Both studio editors have autocomplete features.

6. **Navigation:** Code navigation in both editors is an important feature. You can use keyboard shortcuts keys to navigate to files.

7. **Multi-line cursors:**

   For selecting multiple lines in VS Code, hold option or Alt – cursor.

   In Atom editor, we use Alt – cursor.

8. **Code folding:** It allows you to expand and collapse block code. By folding code, you can focus on specific sections. Both editors support this feature.

9. **Community:** Both code editors currently have large communities and user bases. At the same time, VS Code seems to be more popular, whereas Atom still has a dedicated community of users and developers.

10. **Core features:** VS Code packs in more functionality than Atom or even many other text editors.

11. **Performance:** The performance differences between both come down to a few factors; VS Code is tightly controlled by the set functionality and uses plug-ins to add surface-level features.

Overall, VS Code is a better text editor because of its extensive features and functionality, while Atom users have to increase functionality using plug-ins.

SUBLIME VS VISUAL STUDIO CODE

Sublime Text

It was developed by a Google engineer in 2007. It has a license fee of $80, and it doesn't have a free trial version. VS Code runs on Linux, Windows, and macOS. The latest version of Sublime Text is Version 3.

Fundamental: When you start working, you will get a stripped-back text editor. There is no sidebar, no options to search; there is no option to take you directly to the extension sidebar. In benefits are that it provides a focused layout to help you focus on coding. There is a mini-map on the top right corner to give you an at-a-glance view of your code. If you are newer to text editors, the other features and functionality are harder to find.

Sublime features: If you want, you can install extra plug-ins to give additional functionality. To do that, you need to install a PC (Package Control).

1. We are identifying the different vendor coding within the text.

2. Easy to use and provides many preferences which suit most users' needs.

3. It has many features, which save you a lot of time.

4. It is perfect for working with large datasets.

5. It allows you to customize and choose the particular theme that fits you the best for your programming.

6. It is free to use.

7. It can open and analyze large amounts of text files. Like a CSV file, the sublime can empty it so quickly.

8. You can integrate the compiler with it.

9. Excellent keyboard manager installation and multi-selection options.

10. Most of the editors have text project feature which refers to managing folders and files within Sublime Text. All the files are quickly accessible from the sidebar as soon as you open your project in Sublime.

11. **Snippets:** These features work the same as they do in Visual Studio, but you can also own or install more from extensions.

12. By pressing Ctrl + D all the words will be highlighted within the files; you can also press Ctrl + F to find and replace a word.

NOTEPAD++ VS VISUAL STUDIO CODE

What Is Notepad ++?

If you are a fresher who needs a text editor, Notepad++ is easier to understand. It was released on November 24, 2003, and developed by Dan Ho. Its core features include autosave, syntax highlighting for HTML, PHP, JavaScript, tab support, multiple view, macros, and much more. If core features are not enough, there are also many plug-ins available.

It is specially designed for editing source code. The "++" refers to the increment operator in a programming language such as C, C++, Java, and JavaScript.

Features:

1. Edit multiple files, organized in tabs.

2. A plug-in system for adding features to the software.

3. Advanced find and replace, with support for the regular expression.

4. You can edit any files up to 2 GB in size.

5. Split-screen for editing and viewing multiple files.

Are IDEs Better Than Editors?

IDEs are a more powerful and robust set of tools that are only designed to make coding as simple as possible. It is a code editor with powerful and unique built-in features to simplify and improve your coding process.

Should Beginner Programmers Start Using IDE or Code Editors?

IDEs offer you a simple way of writing and executing a program, but they can be difficult to understand. Beginners might prefer a code editor because they can learn many things, from file extension to debugging.

Above, we have compared VS Code with other editors and also reviewed their fundamental aspects.

What Is the Size of VS Code Exe file?

As we know, VS Code is a lightweight code editor. Its file size is small, less than 100 MB.

Additional Components and Tools

By default, it is a small download and includes a minimum number of components shared across most development workflows. The basic functionality of VS Code like an editor, is better file management, windows management, and preference setting. If you work with larger files, you will be shocked to know that VS Code can efficiently work even with those files.

Type of Components

Commonly used components of VS Code are:

- Git

- Typescript

- Node.js

Additional Tools

It integrates with the existing toolchains. This will enhance your development experience. The tools are:

- Yeoman

- Express

- Yarn

- Mocha

- Gulp

Top Extensions

Extensions allow us to enable additional languages, commands, themes, debuggers, and more. Their growing communities will share top tips to improve your workflow.

- **Code Maid:** It is an open-source Visual Studio extension to dig, clean up, and simplify languages such as HTML, JavaScript, XAML, CSS, LESS, SCSS, C#, C++, F#, VB, XML, ASP, and TypeScript coding.

Features

- **Code Cleaning:** It can run on-demand automatically or on save. It can run on a single file, all opened files, any selection in the entire solution explorer, or the solution explorer.

Critical points for code cleaning:

1. It takes actions on cleanup.

2. It removes unused statements.

3. It sorts using statements.

4. It adds unspecified access modifiers.

5. It removes empty regions.

6. It adds blank line padding.

7. It removes blank lines next to braces.

8. It runs Visual Studio Code formatting.

9. It removes consecutive blank lines.

10. It updates end region tags.

11. It eliminates the end of line whitespace.

12. It visualizes and navigates through the contents of C# and C++ files from a tree hierarchy.

13. It quickly switches between various sorting methods to get a better overview.

14. It types a search filter to find particular items.

15. Drag and drop feature to reorganize the code.

16. Reorganize the layout of members.

17. Generate regions to match automatically.

18. It formats the comments to wrap at a particular column and arranges the tags on separate lines.

19. It helps to join two adjacent lines and highlights sections of code into a single line.

20. It sorts a highlighted section of code alphabetically.

21. It enables, modifies, or disables many aspects of how CodeMaid does its work.

- Remote - SHH Editing Configuration Files

  o It lets you use any of the remote machines with an SSH server for your development environment.
  o This extension will complement the Remote – SSH extension with keyword IntelliSense, syntax colorization, simple snippets while editing SSH configuration files.

Telemetry

VS Code Remote – SSH: Editing Configuration extension files and related extensions collect the telemetry data to help us build a better experience working remotely from Visual Studio Code. We can collect data on which commands are executed. We don't collect any information about image names, paths, etc.

- Add New File

- Place

- Jupyter

- Prettier – code formatter

- Live Server

- Visual Studio IntelliCode

CHAPTER SUMMARY

In this chapter, we have learned briefly about VS Code, IDEs, and code editors. We have also compared the IDEs and editors. Our main motive was to provide some knowledge of VS Code by comparing its pros and cons and also its features with other editors.

CHAPTER 2

Exploring the User Interface

IN THIS CHAPTER

➤ Exploring the user interface of VS Code

➤ What can extensions do?

➤ Installation of PowerShell

➤ User interface

In the previous chapter, we learned about basic features of Visual Studio (VS) Code like its installation, working, and interface, and compared it with other code editors like Atom and Brackets. We also learned about built-in extensions and third-party package installations.

In this chapter, we will learn briefly about Visual Studio Code's user interface, PowerShell, and keyboard shortcuts. So let's get into it.

INTRODUCTION

Visual Studio is an open-source project under stable development.

If you would like to work with prerelease versions of VS Code, you can additionally install the Insiders build in your system. It is an isolated application and its settings and extensions coexist with the regular build on your machine. This will be updated nightly so that you will get the

DOI: 10.1201/9781003311973-2

latest feature updates. This will allow you to test the latest features but still switch to the public release if anything is malfunctioning.

Why Do We Use VS Code over Bracket, Atom, or Another Code Editor?

Visual Studio Code is built-in on electron, which is the same for Atom. So you might assume that Visual Studio Code would end up having these same issues that Atom has. You will be happy to hear that Visual Studio Code is free from many of those issues. If you use Atom for small projects, it works fine. However, as your project files grow, your operating system will become slower and slower because Atom needs a lot of CPU power and has high memory usage. Atom is not for your development. You need something faster. This brings us to Visual Studio Code. When you visit Visual Studio Code's official website to download it, just click "Download", and it will download a zipped folder. On their website, you will learn a lot of useful stuff. You can also watch an introductory video tutorial.

We will cover all the basic aspects of what Visual Studio Code gives you. It gives you some built-in interfaces like Git and debugging that allows you to debug directly from the browser, and it gives you IntelliSense, which is a sort of auto-completion and syntax highlighting tool which is excellent. There's also a whole suite of plug-ins, extensions, and themes (Figure 2.1).

Let's discuss the basics of Visual Studio Code.

The best way of exploring Visual Studio Code hands-on is to open the Get Started Page. You will get a brief overview of VS Code's features and customizations: Help > Get Started (Figure 2.2).

Choose a Walk-through for a self-guided tour through the Visual Studio Code setup, features, and deeper customizations that VS Code offers. If

FIGURE 2.1   Visual Studio Code.

FIGURE 2.2   Get Started page.

you want to improve your code editing skills, open the Interactive Editor Playground. Try Visual Studio Code editing features like multi-cursor editing, IntelliSense, Snippet, and many more.

Commands Line

Visual Studio Code has a more powerful command-line interface that allows you to customize the editor.

Command	Description
code.	Open code with the current directory
code –r	Open the currently active directory in the most recently used window
code - - n	Create a new window
code - -locale= es	Change the language
code - - diff <files> <file2>	Open diff editor
code - - goto package.json:10:5	Open files at specific line and column <file :line [:character]>
code –help	See help options
Code - - disable - extensions	Disable all extensions

Customization

There are so many things that you can do to customize your VS Code.

- **Change your theme:** You can install more themes from the Visual Studio Code extension. Available themes are High Contrast, Dark +

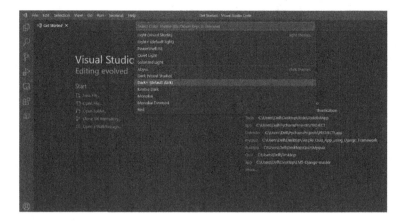

FIGURE 2.3   Change theme.

Default dark, Light + Default light, and many more. Visual Studio has light as well dark themes too.

Keyboard shortcut: Ctrl + K Ctrl + T (Figure 2.3).

Keymaps

You can install a Keymap extension that provides the keyboard shortcuts from your editor to VS Code. Go to Preferences > Keymaps to see the current list on the Marketplace (where you can install amazing extensions). Some of the more popular extensions are:

1. Vim

2. Sublime Text Keymap

3. Python Indent

4. Visual Studio Keymap

5. Atom Keymap

6. Notepad++ keymap

    • Change your keyboard shortcuts.

        Keyboard shortcut: Ctrl + K Ctrl + S (Figure 2.4)

        You can also add and search your key binding shortcut to the keybinding.json files.

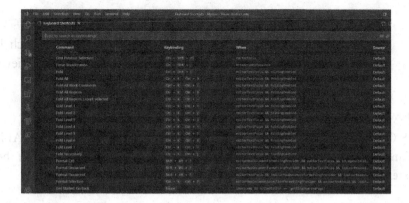

FIGURE 2.4   Keyboard shortcut.

- Tune your settings.

    Keyboard shortcut: Ctrl + , (comma)

    Open your User setting settings.json

    In VS Code by Default, it shows the Setting editor, you can find settings listed below in a search bar:

    Change the tab size level:

    – "editor.tab size": 4

    Change the render whitespace:

    – "editor.renderWhitespace": "selection"

    Change the multi-cursor modifier

    – "editor.multiCursorModifier": "alt"

    Change the auto indent

    – "editor.autoIndent": "full"

    Change the Font size

    – "editor.fontSize": 14

    Change the auto save options

    – "files.autoSave": "off"

- Add JSON validation

- Create snippets

- **Install extensions:** You can search with the search bar or click the more actions button to sort and filter in the extension views (Figure 2.5).

How to Create Your Own Extensions API?

VS Code can be customized and enhanced through the Extension API. Many of the core features of VS Code are built as extensions and use the Extension API.

What Can Extensions Do?

It can change the look of your VS Code with various color or file icon themes, and you can add custom components and views in the User interface and create a web view to display a custom webpage. It supports new programming languages and also supports debugging a specific runtime.

- **Toolbar sidebar:** Keyboard shortcut: Ctrl + B

- **Toggle panel:** Keyboard shortcut: Ctrl + J

- **Zen mode:** Keyboard shortcut: Esc

- **Side by side editing:** Keyboard shortcut: Ctrl + \ (Backward Slash)

- **Switch between editors:** Keyboard shortcut: Ctrl + 1, Ctrl + 2, Ctrl + 3

FIGURE 2.5   Extension view.

- **Move to explorer window:** Keyboard shortcut: Ctrl + Shift + E.

- **Create and open a file:** Keyboard shortcut: Ctrl + clicks

- **Close the currently opened folder:** Keyboard shortcut: Ctrl + F4

- **Navigation history:**

  o **Navigate entire history:** Ctrl + Tab

  o **Navigate back:** Alt + Left

  o **Navigate forward:** Alt + Right

- **Multi-cursor selection:** To add cursors at random positions, select an appointment with your mouse and use shortcuts Alt + Click. To set the pointer above or below the current situations, use their keyboard shortcuts: Ctrl + Alt + Up or Ctrl +Alt + Down.

- **Column/box selection:** You can select blocks of text by holding Shift + Alt while dragging your mouse. With this, you can choose a particular portion of code by holding both keys and then simply dragging your mouse.

- **Vertical rulers:** You can also add vertical column rulers to the editors with the "editor. Rulers" setting, which takes an array of the column positions.

```
{
"editor.rulers":[10,40,10]
}
```

- **Fast scrolling:** Holding the Alt key enables you to fast scroll in your editor. You can quickly scroll your extended code at once. The fast scrolling uses a 5× speed multipliers, but you can control it with the Editor: Fast Scroll settings such as an editor. fastScrollingSensitivity.

- **Copy line up/down:** This command is unbound on Linux because the VS Code editor default key bindings would conflict with Ubuntu key bindings.

- **Keyboard shortcut:** Shift + Alt + Up or by this Shift + Alt + Down.

- **Move line up/down:** Keyboard shortcut: Alt + Up or Alt + Down.

- **Shrink and expand selection:** Keyboard shortcut: Shift + Alt + Left or by Shift + Alt + Right.

- **Go to Symbol in Workspace:** Ctrl + T.

- **Outline view:** This view in the File Explorer shows you the symbols of the currently open files. You can sort the symbol name, category, and position in the files, allowing quick navigation to symbol locations (Figure 2.6).

- **Navigate to a specific line:** Keyboard shortcut: Ctrl + G

- **Undo cursor positions:** Keyboard shortcut: Ctrl + U

- **Trim trailing whitespace:** Keyboard shortcut: Ctrl + Ctrl + X

- **Transform text commands:** You can change the selected text to Uppercase, Lowercase, and Title Case.

- **Code formatting:** Keyboard shortcut: Ctrl + Shift + F (fully document).

- **Keyboard shortcut:** Ctrl + K Ctrl + F (currently selected source code).

- **Code folding:** Keyboard shortcut: Ctrl + Shift + [and Ctrl + Shift +]. You can also unfold/fold regions in the editor keyboard

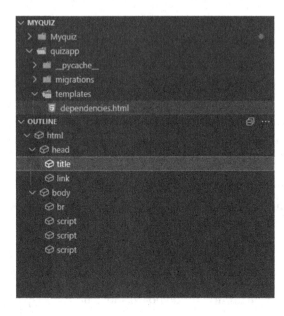

FIGURE 2.6   Outline section.

shortcuts using Unfold All (Ctrl + K Ctrl + J) and Fold All (Ctrl +K Ctrl + 0). You can fold all the block comments with Fold All Block Comments (Ctrl + K Ctrl +/).

- **Select current line:** Keyboard Shortcut: Ctrl + L.

- **Navigate to the beginning and end of the file:** Keyboard short-cut: Ctrl + Home and Ctrl + End.

- **Open Markdown preview:** Keyboard shortcut: Ctrl + Shift + V.

- **Side by side Markdown edits and preview:** Keyboard shortcut: Ctrl + K V.

- **IntelliSense:** Keyboard shortcut: Ctrl + Space. It is used to trig-ger the suggestions widgets.

- **Peek keyboard shortcut:** Alt + F12. You can use the context menu instead.

- **Go to definitions:** Select a symbol, then type F12. You can use the context menu instead or by using Ctrl + Click. We also have one Go tab in the menu bar of the VS Code.

- **Find all reference view:** You can select a symbol, then type Shift + Alt + F12 to open the references view showing all your files' symbols in a dedicated view.

- **Rename symbol:** You can select the particular text and then press F2. On the other hand, you can use the context menu.

- **Emmet syntax:** VS Code supports Emmet syntax in their editor. Examples:

```
//Type this and hit enter. You will get the
output
nav>ul>li.

//Output
<nav>
 <ul>
  <li></li>
 </ul>
</nav>
```

- **Git integration:** Keyboard shortcut: Ctrl + Shift + G. It comes with Visual Studio Code "out-of-the-box." You can install other SCM providers from the Extension Marketplace.

- **Review pane:** Keyboard shortcut F7 and Shift + F7.

- **Branches:** It quickly switches between Git branches via the status bar.

INSTALL THE POWERSHELL EXTENSION

PowerShell Extension Services is an application programming interface that makes the PowerShell environment portable across various host applications, even on non-Windows platforms.

Start VS Code and click view > command palette (or by pressing Ctrl + Shift + P) to open the command palette. Enter ext install PowerShell, down to PowerShell entry, and hit Enter to install the PowerShell Language Support for Visual Studio Code Extension (Figure 2.7).

Some of the features of PowerShell are:

- Local debugging in primary console

- Syntax highlighting

- Code snippets

- IntelliSense code completion

BASIC USER INTERFACE

Let's have a look over the Visual Studio Code User Interface. First, we will talk about its basic layout.

Visual Studio Code comes with a simple layout that will maximize the size of the editor. The UI (User Interface) is divided into main five areas (Figure 2.8):

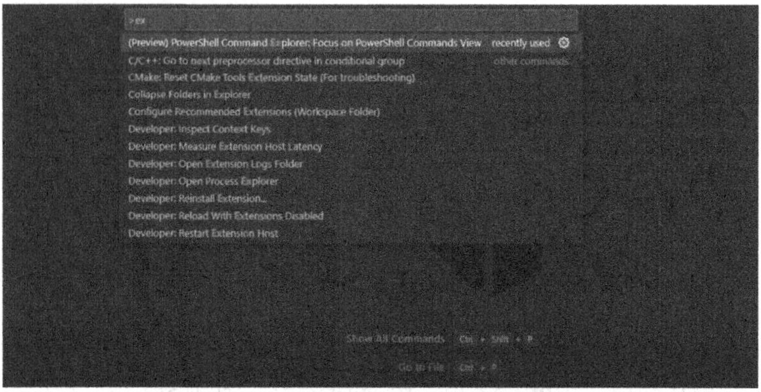

FIGURE 2.7   PowerShell in Visual Studio Code.

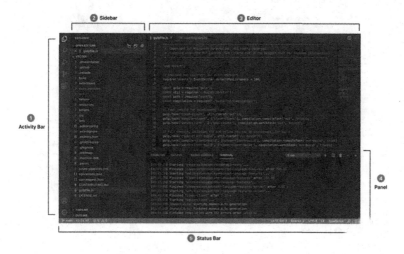

FIGURE 2.8   Visual Studio Code.

1. **Editor:** The central regions where you can edit your files. You can open a lot of editors as you want side by side.

2. **Side bar:** This bar contains various views like Explorer, Search, Git, Debug, Extensions, Error and Warnings, Split Editors, and Language Mode.

3. **Status bar:** It contains information about the opened project and files you edit.

4. **Activity bar:** It locates on the left-hand side. This will let you switch between views and gives.

5. **Panels:** Here, you can see output or errors, warning, debug information, or an integrated terminal. You can increase the size of the panel and also move left to right. The folder, layout, and open files and folder are preserved. It opens in the previous state it was in last (Figure 2.9).

   - **View container:** These are the part of the activity bar; each container has a unique icon. With the contributes. You can add new view containers next to the five built-in views in the sidebar.

     The File Explorer is one of the Views in Visual Studio Code. There are various views for other options too:

   - **Search:** It provides you a global search and replaces it across your open folder.

FIGURE 2.9   Items inside the various containers.

FIGURE 2.10   You can open any view using the View: Open View command.

- **Source control:** Visual Studio Code includes the Git source control by default.

- **Run:** Visual Studio Code run and debug view displays variables, breakpoints, and call stacks.

- **Extension:** Install and manage your attachments within VS Code.

- **Custom views:** View contributed by extensions (Figure 2.10).

  Icon specifications

- Icon size should be 24*24 and centered.

- It should use a single color.

- Its icon should be in SVG.

    All the icons default inherit the following state styles:

State	Opacity
Default	60%
Hover	100%
Active	100%

- **Views:** These are the containers of the content displayed in the sidebar or panel. It can contain tree views, custom views, and also show view actions. The user can rearrange it into other views, activity bar, and panels (Figure 2.11).

- View toolbar

- Side toolbar

- Panel toolbar

FIGURE 2.11   Way to search.

- **Status bar item:** It sits at the bottom of VS Code and displays information and actions that relate to your current workspace. It has two groups: The primary group (left) and the Secondary group (right). Items on the left side are statuses (problem/warnings, sync) and on the right side, we get language, spacing, feedback.

- **Tree view:** The contributes. View points help you to add a new view that displays in any of the view containers.

- **Web view:** It is a highly customizable view built using HTML/CSS/JavaScript. This will display next to the text editor in the editor group areas. The web view API allows you to create fully customizable views within Visual Studio Code. For example, it can build up a complex user interface beyond what the VS Code native APIs support. Create view panel is used to create a web view. The web view panel will be shown in VS Code as a separate editor. It will make them for displaying custom UI and custom visualizations.

Various sidebar icons represent different functionality (Figure 2.12).

1. **Explorer:** Like other code editors, VS Code has the familiar user interface and layout of an explorer on the left corner of the screen. It will show you all the files and folders you have to access for some

FIGURE 2.12   Sidebar icons.

purpose, and the editor on the top right offers your currently opened files' content.

After opening your folder in VS Code, you can do many things from here:

- Create, delete, and rename files and folder names.

- Using mouse drag and drop, you can move files and folders.

2. **Search:** It will scan your entire document in your current workspace using a matching processor regular expressions. Open search bar shortcut VS Code,

- Search file (using Ctrl + P)

   If you know the name of your file, there is no longer a need to go into File Explorer. By pressing Ctrl + P, Visual Studio Code will automatically look into your current workspace and display the similar that contains the name you just wrote (Figure 2.13).

- Search for the symbol (using Ctrl + T)

   The name of a private function that you do not know its exact location for will help you. Simply hit Ctrl + T in the Command Palette or manually type the # prefix in the command palette bar (Figure 2.14).

- Search local symbol (using CTRL + SHIFT + O)

   The same as the previous search for a symbol, you can also open the command palette and just Type @.or

   By adding: you can group them that make your work simple like @: in the command palette (Figure 2.15).

- Search by reference (using Shift + F12)

   You should know about this feature in VS Code. It is implemented in such a way that makes searching for references so fast. It will show all the references of the current variation of the function.

   If you do not want to perform these shortcuts using the keyboard, you can simply select that variable or function, then click the right button on the mouse and you see all the preferences related to the search.

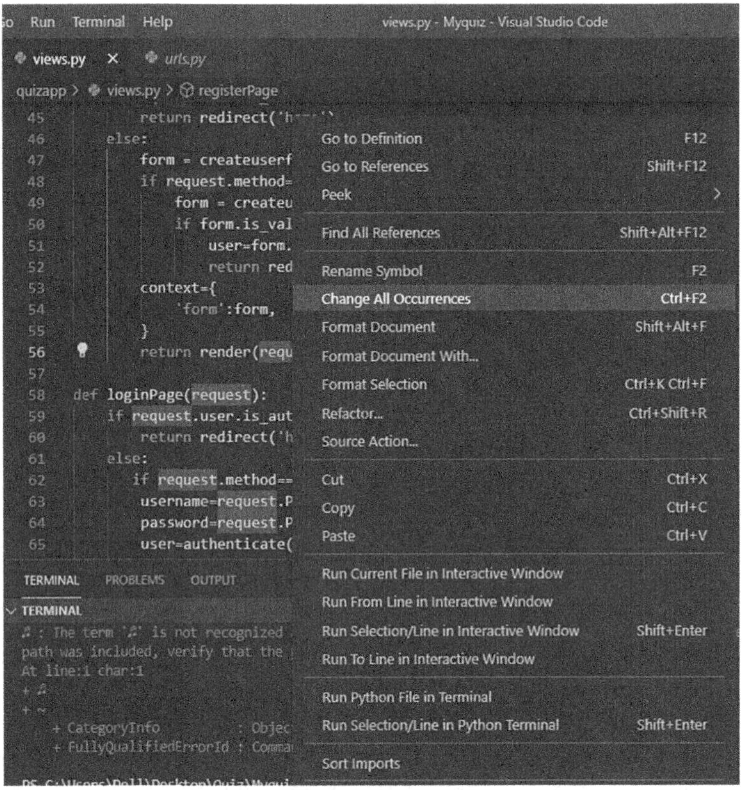

FIGURE 2.13   Way to search using command palette.

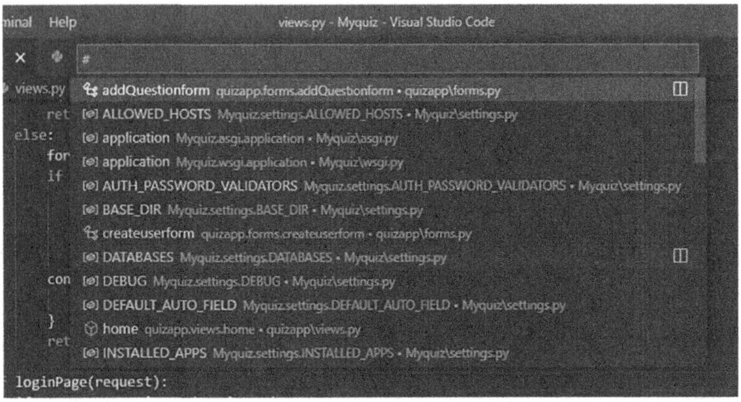

FIGURE 2.14   Searching by symbol using # prefix in the command palette.

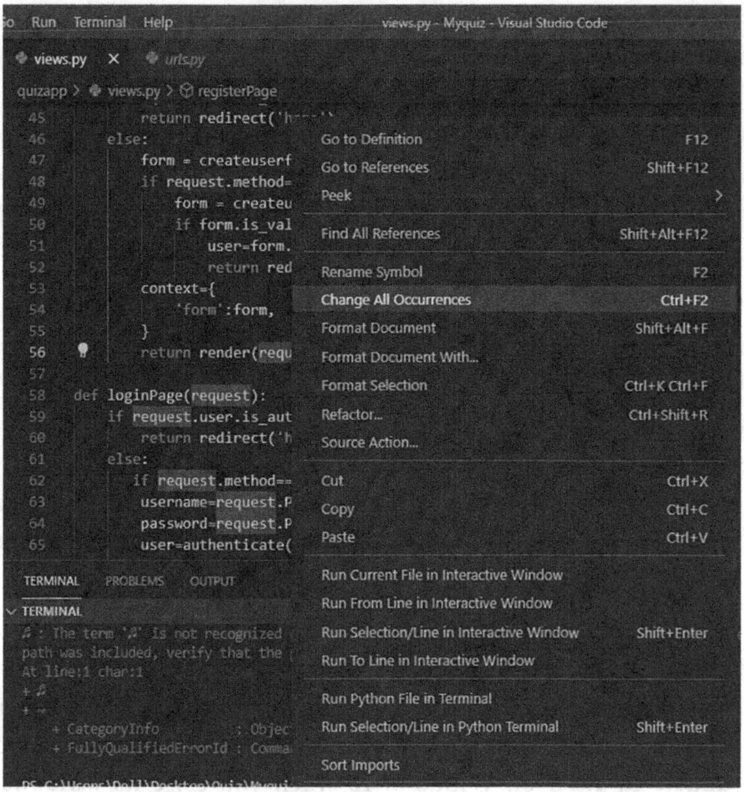

FIGURE 2.15   Searching by symbol using @ prefix in the command palette.

3. **Git:** VS Code has built-in features, namely with Git. The third icon in the sidebar is known for Git (it looks like a split in the road). It will make your workflow better and more efficient. We have a separate section where we will discuss everything about Git integration.

4. **Debug:** It will perform live debugging with standard features: variable, breakpoints, watch, etc.

5. **Extensions:** It provides a shortcut method to the command palette that allows you to manage your attachments.

6. **Testing:** It supports running and debugging tests for your installed extensions. These will run inside a remarkable instance of VS Code named the Extension Development Host and have full access to the VS Code API (Application Programming Interface).

7. **References:** It is available on the sidebar of the second last icon or by right-clicking on that particular element to reference.

There are two more icons on the bottom of the sidebar, which are named Account and Manage.

1. **Accounts:** You can perform setting sync that lets you share your Visual Studio Code configuration, such as settings and key bindings, and install extra extensions across your machines so that you can work with your favorite setup. Then you get Turn on settings sync options like below (Figure 2.16).

   They will ask you to sign in with your Github or Microsoft account to get your favorite configurations all the time. You can also add your Outlook and Azure accounts to it.

2. **Manage:** In manage, you can get some direct options as you can easily open the command palette, settings, extensions, and themes. Manage your workspace and check the latest updated version for VS Code (Figure 2.17).

ADDITIONAL OPTIONS

- **Notification examples:** This will only happen after the user run an update version command. Visual Studio Code will automatically update by itself on Windows 10 when you close its windows. By manually, you can check it from the manage icon (which looks like a settings icon). Manage > Check for updates…

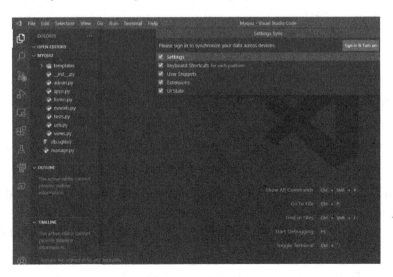

FIGURE 2.16   Showing account icon.

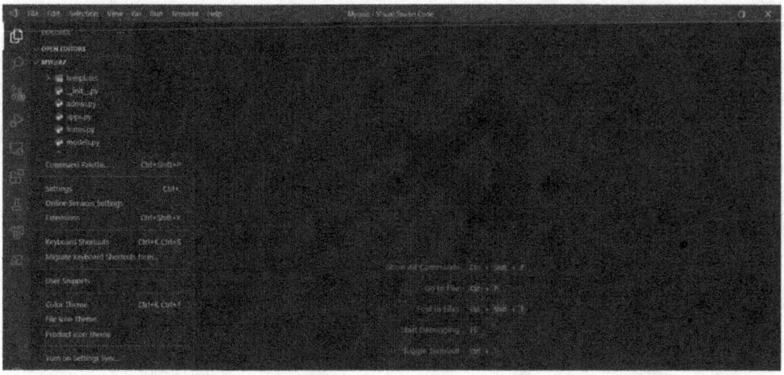

FIGURE 2.17   Showing manage icon.

- **Progress notification:** It is used when you need to display an unde-termined timeframe for setting up an environment.

Editing of multiple files at once: You can open many editors side by side vertically and horizontally. There are multiple ways of opening other edi-tor windows to the side of the currently existing one:

1. By pressing the Alt key and clicking on any file in the explorer.

2. Click Ctrl + \ (backward slash) to split the active editor into two.

3. For multiple splitting, you can select the files and hit Ctrl +Enter.

Figures 2.18–2.20 make clear a few of the differences.

- For Multiple Screens splitting in VS Code see Figure 2.18.

- For Single Screens splitting in VS Code see Figure 2.19.

- For the Screen Splitting Button in VS Code see Figure 2.20.

- By default, editors will open files to the right side of the active one.

Minimap

A code outline gives you a high-level overview of your code, beneficial for navigation and code understanding. It is shown on the top right side of the editor. You can also move the minimap to the left side or disable it com-pletely in the settings "editor. minimap.side" : "left" or "editor.minimap.s ide" : "false" in your workspace setting.

FIGURE 2.18   Multiple screens splitting.

FIGURE 2.19   Single screens splitting.

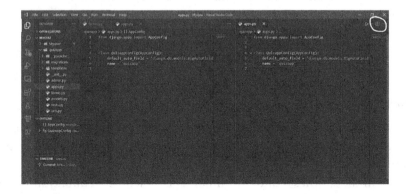

FIGURE 2.20   Screen splitting button.

How can you open this setting? There are two different scopes for setting.

1. **User setting:** This setting can apply globally to any instance of VS Code.

2. **Workspace setting:** This setting can only apply to that workspace that is currently opened.

On Windows/Linux, settings location is File > Preference > Settings.

On macOS, settings location is Code > Preference > Settings (Figure 2.21).

You can change the settings from here. When you modify the scenes, it is reloaded by the VS Code. This setting helps share the project setting across a team. Each location can edit by dropdown, an input, or by checkbox.

Multi-selection

You can select various files in the File Explorer and open the Editors view to run actions (Drop, Delete, Drag, and so on). Use the Ctrl/cmd key with a click to select single files and Shift + click to select a range.

Outline View

It is a separate section at the bottom of the File Explorer. When it expands, it will show the tree view of the currently active files. This view has different sorts by modes such as Position, Name, and Type (Figure 2.22).

FIGURE 2.21 Setting screen.

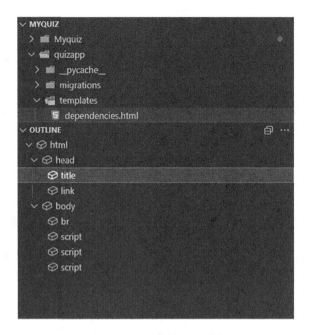

FIGURE 2.22   Outline section.

Several Outline view settings allow us to enable/disable icons and control the errors and warning displays.

- **Outline.Icons:** It toggles rendering outline elements with icons.

- **Outline.problems.enabled:** It shows errors and warnings on the outline element.

- **Outline.problem.badges:** It is used to toggle using badges for errors and warnings.

- **Outline.problem.colors:** It is used to toggle color for errors and warnings.

Activity Bar

This bar is on the left side, which helps you switch between views quickly, or you can also reorder the idea by dragging and dropping them on the bar or remove a View entirely just by clicking right (Figure 2.23).

Command Palette

It is an interactive list bound to Ctrl + Shift + P (brings up to command palette) whose only purpose is to execute commands (Figure 2.24).

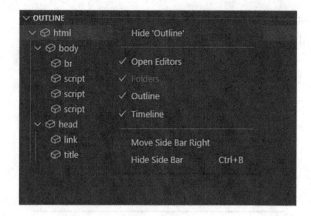

FIGURE 2.23 Hide activity bar.

FIGURE 2.24 Command palette.

How to Open the Command Palette in the VS Code

1. Launch VS Code on Windows.

2. Press "Ctrl + Shift + P".

3. Another way to open the command palette is to click on View > command palette.

You will learn about all the essential commands that developers using VS Code should know.

Some Useful Shortcuts Keys for VS Code in Windows

The shortcut keys for the VS Code editor are as follows:

Shortcut Key	Description
Shift + Ctrl + Enter Button	Insert line above
Ctrl + Enter Button	Insert line below
Shift + Ctrl + K	Delete line
Shift + Alt + Up Arrow Button	Copy line up
Shift + Alt + Down Arrow Button	Copy line down
Alt + Up Arrow Button	Move line up
Alt + Down Arrow Button	Move line down

Commonly Used Commands

Shortcut Key	Description
Ctrl + Shift + P, F1	Show command palette
Ctrl + P	Search file name
Ctrl + Shift + N	Open new window
Ctrl + Shift + W	Close current window
Ctrl + , (Comma)	Open user settings
Ctrl + K + Ctrl (separate button) + S	Open keyboard shortcuts

Navigation

Shortcut Key	Description
Ctrl + T	Show all symbols
Ctrl + G	Go to Line number (Example:12)
Ctrl + P	Go to file (whatever you will type)
Ctrl + Shift + O	Go to the symbol (@containers)
Shift + F8	Go to the previous error or warning
F8	Go to the next error or warning
Alt + left arrow button/right arrow button	Go back/forward

Zen Mode

It lets you focus on your code by hiding all the User Interfaces except the editor screen (there will be no activity bar, status bar, side bar, panel). It can be toggled using the View menu, command palette, or by the short-cuts keys Ctrl + K Z. To exit Zen mode click double Esc. The given settings can further tune it:

1. zenMode.hideStatusBar

2. zenMode.zhide tabs

3. zenMode.fullScreen

4. zenMode.restore

5. zenMode.centerLayout

Centered Editor Layout

It allows you to center align the editor area. This is useful when we are working with a single editor on a large screen. You can also use the sashes on the side to resize the view.

Tabs

Visual Studio Code has various tabs options. It shows open items with tabs in the title rare above the editor. You can quickly drag and drop to reorder the tabs. If you do not want to use tabs, you can disable this feature in the user set as a workbench. editor.showTabs setting to false:

"workbench. editor.showTabs" : false

Tab Ordering

By default, the new tabs are added to the right of the previous tabs; you can also control this part of the Tab to appear with the workbench. Editor. Open positioning setting;

For, example, "workbench.editor.openPositoning": "left".

Editor Groups

When the user splits an editor using the Split Editor or Open to the Side commands, a new editor holds various items. You can open any editor side by side vertically and horizontally (Figure 2.25).

Grid Layout

Default editor groups are shown in vertical columns, but with this feature, you can easily arrange editor groups in any form, both vertically and horizontally. You can also create empty editor groups. The default

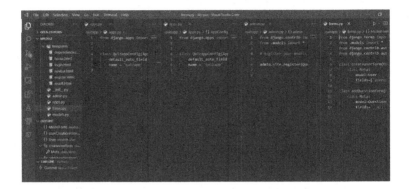

FIGURE 2.25   Multiple screens splitting.

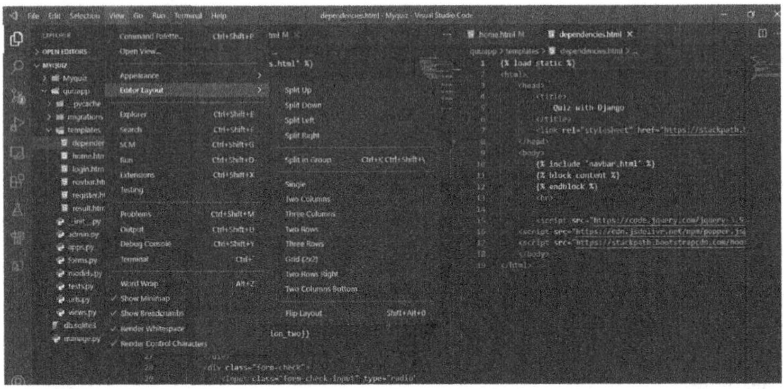

FIGURE 2.26   Grid layout.

behaviors of the editor will close the group by closing the last editor in setting:

"workbench. editor.closeEmptyGroups": "false"

The editor opens to the right side by default of the active editor. If you want to open that editor below to the active one, you must configure the new setting workbench. editor,openSideBySideDirection: down (Figure 2.26).

There are various commands for adjusting the editor layout with the keyboard. Drag and drop are the fastest way to split the editor if you want to use the mouse.

Some Useful Keyboard Shortcuts

Shortcuts	Description
Ctrl + PageDown	Go to the right editor
Ctrl + Page Up	Go to the left editor
Ctrl + Tab	Open the last editor in the editor group list
Ctrl + 1	Go to left most editor group
Ctrl + 2	Go to center editor group
Ctrl + 3	Go to rightmost editor group
Ctrl + F4	Close the active editor
Ctrl + K W	Close all the editors in the group
Ctrl+ K Ctrl + W	Close all editors

Some Keyboard Rules

Each rule consists of:

1. A key that defines the pressed keys.

2. A command contains the identifiers of the command to execute.

3. An optional when clause containing a Boolean expression will be evaluated depending on the current context.

Theming

In Visual Studio Code, there are three types of themes:

1. **Color Theme:** It is mapping from both UI Component Identifier and Text Token Identifier to colors. It allows you to apply your favorite color to both vs. Code UI Components and the editor's text.

2. **File Icon Theme:** It is mapping files type/files name to images. Icons are across the VS Code UI in place, such as File Explorer.

3. **Product Icon Theme:** It is a set of icons used through the UI, from the sidebar, the Activity bar, Status bar to the editor.

Declarative Language Features

These add essential text editing support for a programming language such as bracket matching, syntax highlighting, auto-completion, etc. for more advanced features like IntelliSense or debugging.

Few important terms that include in the VS Code editor interface.

- **Multiple cursors:** Visual Studio Code lets you work on various sections of a file at one time. This is user-friendly when you need to perform many uniform changes. By holding the Alt key and clicking on the text editor's respective area you can create a new cursor. From that point forward, any changes made via keyboard input will be applied to all selected cursor positions. It is possible to select multiple sections in your code.

- **Use of the command palette to control VS Code:** Press Ctrl + P to open the Palette without any input from the mouse; this puts you into navigation mode and displays a list of open files. Entering a few letters will filter the opened files and the files in opened folders will show the desired result. This means you can quickly jump between files. If you are inside a project that supports IntelliSense, this functionality will even search detected symbols.

  Additional modes allow you to control many areas of VS Code. You can display a list of all combinations by entering "?". It's worth memorizing and using the various options. They often help you in keeping your hand away from the mouse, thus improving your productivity.

- **Selecting a language for a file:** Visual Studio Code supports syntax highlighting for many programming languages like JavaScript, Python, HTML, CSS, etc. To select a language for the active file, either run the command Change Language Mode or click the status bar's current language area in the bottom right corner, which will open a list of available languages to make a selection.

- **AutoSave:** Visual Studio Code supports the AutoSave feature in the editor. This feature automatically and immediately saves the current document after each change. This is mainly useful for web-related files. You are not required to click on Save or press Ctrl + S, and all files are up-to-date when clicking refresh in the browser after a specific interval of time. You just need to use automated tasks that keep repeating as a file gets changed (for example, TypeScript to JavaScript) as this can cause a heavy load on CPU power.

  AutoSave can be enabled and disabled in the workspace settings using the option "files.autoSave". It is also possible to slow down (delay) AutoSave operations for a specified amount of time by setting "files.autoSave" to "after delay" and setting "files.autoSave" to the desired delay in milliseconds, e. g.:

"files.autoSave": "after delay" "files.autosave delay": 1000

- **Hiding undesired folders:** If you have worked on files or folders that you never edit within opened folders, you can hide those files or folders in the File Explorer view. For example, suppose you have your node js project, and it has a node_modules folder in it, to hide the file or folder or any pattern file, you just need to reference them in the "files. Exclude" option in your user or workspace settings. User—the workspace settings to hide those entries file or folder only within the active project.

- **Hiding search results:** Visual Studio Code offers a straightforward search function for all active files. When we iterate through the search results, it can be helpful to hide results from that list for files you have already checked. If something within the found files needs to be modified, this can help keep focus on areas you have already touched. Under each filename, Visual Studio Code displays the number of search hits within that file. When you hover over that number with your mouse pointer, you will see a cross which you can click on to hide that filename from the list.

- **Re-inserting regex matches:** Visual Studio Code search functionality helps your regular expressions. This will allow you to find not only text but also whole syntactical constructs. Its real power lies in combining it with the replace function, which not only inserts static text but can also relate to the results of the regular expression search.

- **Emmet snippets:** For all of their excellent readability, HTML and XML are often hard to code in both for beginners. To enhance the creation of such HTML and XML documents, Visual Studio Code supports the extension named Emmet snippets. These Emmet snippets are expressions similar to CSS, which are converted to, for example, HTML or XML after pressing the tab key.

  In its simplest form, just a single element would be created. For example, if you write "HTML" to a file that VS Code easily recognizes as an HTML file, and after that press the tab key twice, this text is being replaced with "<html> to </html>". The cursor is positioned between the two tags.

But the Emmet snippets can do a lot more. There is a set of constructs that are supported by Emmet snippets: If you press the tab key after entering "li*5", VS Code will insert five "<li></li>" fragments.

- **Keyboard Shortcut Chords:** Like any other IDE or code editor like Visual Studio, Visual Studio Code supports many keyboard shortcut chords. This means that the editor is awaiting a second keyboard shortcut after entering the first keyboard shortcut. This allows you to the grouping of similar commands.

  For example, you can change the searching options in a file from Ctrl + F shortcuts to Ctrl + F + Ctrl + F and the global search in all files using this Ctrl + F + Ctrl + G. In the keybindings.json file, using blank space, the keyboard shortcuts for the chord must be separated.

- **Markdown Preview:** Markdown is a simple markup language for authoring formatted file text. Even if markdown is legible in its original shape, it is easier to read when displayed as an appropriately formatted document, especially external resources like images and such.

  Visual Studio offers a markdown preview function that can be opened beneath the text. VS Code is using the GitHub Flavoured Markdown, which offers additional parts over the original markdown format. This comes in handy, especially for GitHub "read me" documents. Using Ctrl+Shift+V, you can switch between Markdown and Preview. The chord Ctrl+K, V opens the preview to the side. Alt + Z toggles word wrapping, which can also be done using the View menu.

- **Visualizing CSS Selectors:** CSS selectors introduce any type of CSS clause. They may define what HTML elements to style with the following properties. Selectors can become pretty complicated, and it is because sometimes you just might not be so familiar with one of them that you are using less often.

  Visual Studio Code solves all the problems by presenting a presentation for the current selector that shows what HTML elements would have to be like to be covered by the selector.

- **The updated version of Dependencies in package.json file in vs. code:** When you are working node.js project, package.json contains a couple of sections that describe as dependencies. For every dependency, more than one version number can be specified.

  This Visual Studio Code editor allows you to display module information by simply moving the mouse cursor pointer over one of the dependencies to show the name, a short description, and the latest version number for that module.

  You can add new dependencies for your modules using shortcut Ctrl + Spacebar.

- **Git Quick Change Information:** If you are working on a Git repository, then VS Code offers a clean way of comparing the version you are working on with the active one in the repository using Git Compare View.

  VS Code even shows code changes when you simply edit some file that is under Git source control. At the left-hand side of the editor, right between row numbers and code, you will find indicators for changed, deleted, and new rows. All the changes are indicated with the help of red, blue, and green colors. All these color has some meanings.

- **Refreshing Git-Views:** Visual Studio Code can also use the external program Git to track changes in any Git directories. Sometimes you will face a view that is not entirely up-to-date or even mess up. To refresh that messy view, use the refresh icons located at the Git header or the status bar.

- **Git Inline Comparison:** Having Visual Studio Code display changes in a file compared to the current Git version opens a view that shows the changing result side by side.

  However, Visual Studio also offers a path to display all the changes in a single code window. The sub-menu Switch to Inline View from the header's "…" menu to get to the Git inline comparison.

- **Comparing Files:** This code offers you a great viewport to make the comparison between two files. You will often get the view when using Git in the VS Code. If you click any of the file names within the Git area, all alterations to the previous file will be displayed.

But VS Code can do more clearly than that. It can compare one file with any other file. You can get the comparative view using the command palette by clicking Ctrl + Shift + P or the explorer area context menu. For the command palette, you will execute Files: Compare Active File Within... and choose a file you wish to compare to the currently opened file. Take the context menu route, activate the context menu for a file in the explorer view, and click Select for Comparison. If you finally start the context menu for another file, you can click on Compare with ,<First File>'. Any of the two options launch the comparison view.

- **Extensions:** Visual Studio Code comes with a lot of built-in features also with a bunch of functionality. But one of the best best of all components is to create new functionality and easily share it with the rest of the world. Extensions are developed with TypeScript or JavaScript or in many other languages. They can be shared in the Visual Studio Code Extension Marketplace (you can check the attachment by using Ctrl + Shift +X). Others who use vs. code can search them in the Marketplace and install available extensions with no more than a single mouse click. Using this way, VS Code can be extended by third parties.

- **Configuration of PHP language for Visual Studio Code:** Visual Studio Code supports many language syntaxes highlighting not only for PHP, but it helps you to include help texts and further parameter information for many of its functions. But VS Code can also provide validation source code, and display errors live.

- **Storage Locations:** Visual Studio saves files to various locations within the file system. It can become comfortable to know what is being stored or what to not where in the settings.

- **Keyboard Shortcuts and Code Snippets:** VS Code Settings are easily obtained using the command palette. They all are stored in settings.json. It depends on what operating system you use. This file can be found at separate locations. In this folder, you will additionally find keybindings.json at this exact location and also a folder named snippets.

- **Synchronizing Settings and Extensions:** Visual Studio Code does not have some functionality that supports the synchronizing settings and installed extensions between various systems. But while all settings are being stored in files and folders, it is a must to synchronize those.

Services like One Drive or Dropbox can provide machine-independent storage get from anywhere. Another easy way is to replace the folders with new synchronized folders. Of course, you must first move all settings and extensions to those new folders.

- **Deactivating Crash Reports:** When Visual Studio Code hangs and crashes, it sends a report to Microsoft to help improve the product features. If you are unwilling to create and send such a report, you can set the option value of the "telemetry.enableCrashReporter" option in your workspace settings from true to false. Then you need to restart your VS Code needs for the change to take effect.

- **Deactivating Telemetry:** VS Code collects data on how it is used. This data is sent to Microsoft, where it is used to improve VS Code. If you are unwilling to create and send such a report, you can set the option value of "telemetry. enable telemetry" in your workspace settings from true to false. Then you need to restart your VS Code needs for the change to take effect.

- **Navigating Files in the Editor:** The VS Code editor is a powerful tool that mainly shows its strength when using keyboard shortcuts for exploring. Many of the shortcuts can be retrieved from VS Code menu, where they are listed right beside the menu item captions, from the command palette, or after pressing Ctrl + Shift + P.

  A special shortcut is Ctrl + E or which can be used with Ctrl + Tab. It opens up a list of recently used files that were opened in the current code editor. Navigating this list is quickly done by repetitive use of the shortcut. On the other hand, press the Shift key to traverse the list in the reverse direction. Alternatively, you can also use the arrow keys on your keyboard.

- **Opening Files in Dedicated Editor Windows:** VS Code supports opening files in an editor window side by side to the existing active one. To do the same, simply hold down the Ctrl key while clicking on a file name in the explorer area. File lists come with an icon to the right.

- **Customizing Keyboard Shortcuts:** Using keyboard shortcuts makes you more productive than often having to use your mouse or lift your hand away from the keyboard. In the upcoming chapter, we will discuss the critical binding in detail.

- **Keyboard Shortcuts:** There are various shortcuts available in the VS Code editor. A few of them are given below.

Shortcuts	Description
Alt + Z	Toggle Word Wrap
Ctrl + P	Quick Open
Ctrl +	Tab Navigate Recent Files
Ctrl + 1/2/	3 Focus First/Second/Third Editor
Ctrl + W	Close Active Editor
Ctrl+/	Comment in/out Line(s)
Ctrl + Shift + K	Delete Line(s)
Ctrl + Click	Open File from Explorer to the Side
Alt + C	Find Case Sensitive
Alt+ W	Find Whole Word
Ctrl + K,	F12 Open Declarations to the Side
Ctrl + D	Add Selection to next Find Match
Ctrl + K, Ctrl + D	Move Selection to next Find Match
Alt + Down	Move Line Down

- **Changing the UI Language:** To launch Visual Studio Code in a supported language of your choice, edit locale.json to open it by pressing F1 and Configure language. Set the value for "locale" to the desired locale example "en-us" for the US, "fr-fr" for France, etc., "de-de" for Germany,

- **Enforcing Word Wrap in the Editor:** Using Alt+Z in an editor toggles Word Wrap. The VS Code has a setting in settings.json that looks at the editor's line length: The default value for "editor.wrappingColumn" is 300, meaning a long line will not wrap before exceeding 300 characters.

CHAPTER SUMMARY

In this entire chapter, we have learned about the Visual Studio Code's user interfaces, basic terms and layout, some helpful keyboard shortcuts that you should know, and command-line shortcuts.

CHAPTER 3

Files, Folders, and Projects

IN THIS CHAPTER

➢ The basic overview of files, folders, and project

➢ Files

➢ Folders

➢ Projects

In the previous chapter, we briefly discussed the user interface of the Visual Studio Code and its layout, PowerShell, and keyboard shortcuts.

In this chapter, we will see how we can work with files, folders, and projects in VS Code.

THE BASICS OF VISUAL STUDIO CODE

Visual Studio Code is a code editor like many editors. It adopts a standard user interface and layout of an explorer on the left side, which shows all the files and folders you have access to, and an editor on the right, showing the content of the files which you have opened.

In addition, there are several unique features in the VS Code user interface; and this chapter will describe these features.

DOI: 10.1201/9781003311973-3

FILES, FOLDERS, AND PROJECTS

Visual Code Editor is based on files and folders – you can get anything immediately by opening files or folders in VS Code. The editor can read and take benefits of various project files defined by the server framework and platform. For example, if the folder you have opened in VS Code contains one or more project files, VS Code will read these files and use them to provide extra functionality, such as IntelliSense, in the editor.

Basic Layout

VS Code comes with a built-in and straightforward layout that maximizes the coding space for the editor while leaving ample space to browse and access the whole context of the folder or project. The VS Code user interface is divided into four areas:

1. **Editor:** This is the main area where you can edit your files. You can open up to three editors side by side using split tools or by using a keyboard shortcut.

2. **Side Bar:** This contains different views like the explorer to assist you while working on your project. Search will assist you in finding various files and folders or text within the files.

3. **Status Bar:** This will provide information about opened projects. It sits at the bottom of the VS Code workbench. When you extend the status bar, you can display information and the user interface in four regions. Actions will relate to the current workspace. The four regions are (1) the feedback region which allows you to display text and highlight the text tool; (2) the progress bar which shows incremental progress for short-running operations such as saving files; (3) the animation region which displays a looped animation for loop-running operations; and (4) the designer region which provides the line and column number for the cursor's location.

4. **Menu Bar:** On the top of the editor's screen, press the Alt button to make it visible and then in the View > Appearance > Show Menu Bar. Another way is to press Alt.

Each time you start your VS Code, it will open up in the same state as you closed it. VS Code will help you to preserve the currently opened folder, layout, and files. Instead of placing files in different tabs, VS Code allows up to three editors together side by side.

This will help reduce the overhead of managing several tabs but restricts the number of files you can work with. The explorer view maintains tabs as a list of working files allowing you quick access to files you need.

Note: You can move the side bar to the right hand side (View > Move Sidebar) or toggle its visibility with "workbench.action.toggleSidebarVisi bilty".

Working with Files

At the topmost of the explorer is a section labeled MYQUIZ. This is a list of your currently active files. These are files you have opened before in VS Code that you are working on. For example, files will be shown here in the section if you do any of these steps:

- Make a change to a file.

- Double-click a file in the explorer.

- Open a file that is not part of the current folder.

The working with files section is similar to tabs that you may be familiar with within the rest of the code editor or IDEs. Just by clicking a file in the working files, it becomes active in VS Code (Figure 3.1).

Once you open a file, you can remove single files from the working files section or remove all the files from the operating files section with the help of the Close All Files action.

Note: Type "workbench.files.action.workingFilesPicker" to navigate the list of current working files from the file picker without having the explorer shown.

The working with files list is a Visual Studio Code extension that shows a vertically stacked list of the files that have been opened in the editor in a tool window. This extension doesn't have a digital signature, but has some features:

- Sort by document project name

- File type icons

- Ability to pin files

- Sort by document name/recently used order

- Group by project

- Automatically assign list entry color based on project

FIGURE 3.1   Working with files.

Configuring the Editor

Visual Studio Code gives you many various options to configure your editor. You can also set options globally through user settings or as per project using the workspace setting. Setting values are kept in a setting.json file.

Steps to Go to Setting Options
There are two kinds of setting as follows:

1. User settings

2. Workspace settings

Go to the menu bar for user settings, select Files > Preferences > User Settings to edit your user settings.json files (or press (workbench.action.show commands), type user, and press Enter).

For workspace settings, go to the menu bar, then select Files > Preferences > Workspace Settings to edit your user settings.json files (or press (workbench.action.show commands), type user, and press Enter).

You will see the VS Code default settings on the left side of the window and your editable settings.json on the right. You can quickly look and copy settings from default settings. After editing your settings, type (workbench.action.files.save) to save your changes. This change will take effect immediately.

Save/AutoSave

By default, Visual Studio Code requires an explicit action to save your changes in your workspace, "workbench.action.files.save". However, it is easy to turn on autosave options, saving your changes after a configured delay or when focus leaves the editor.

How to Enable AutoAave in Visual Studio Code

1. Firstly open Visual Studio Code in your system and open settings by pressing "Ctrl +" if you are using a windows machine, or press "Cmd +" if you are on a Mac machine.

2. **Now, in the search bar type "auto save" and in the "files.auto-Save": "off"** list select the option to "afterdelay" like "files.autoSave": "afterdelay".

3. **After that, in the "files.autoSave":** "after delay" list, set your desired delay time in milliseconds after which Visual Studio Code will automatically save the changes in a file. "files. autosave delay": 1000. In our case, the delay time is 1000 milliseconds (Figure 3.2).

To configure autosave, open user settings or workspace settings and find the locations:

• **Files.autoSave:** Can have the default value "off" to disable autosave, "after delay" to save files after a configured delay, and "on focus change" to save files when focus moves out of the editor.

FIGURE 3.2   Enabling autosave in VS Code.

- **file.autoSaveDelay:** Configures the delay in milliseconds when files. autoSave is configured to "after delay".

What Is VS Code "Workspace"?

A VS Code "workspace" is a group of one or more folders opened in the VS Code window. Generally, you will have a single folder opened depending on the workflow, and you can include more folders using advanced configurations called multi-root workspaces.

Multi-root workspaces are an advanced capability of VS Code that allow you to configure multiple separate folders. Instead of opening a folder as a workspace, you will open a <name>. code-workspace JSON file that lists all the folders of the workspace.

The difference between having a folder opened versus opening a .code-workspace file can be subtle. For example, the root folder of the file explorer shows an extra suffix named (Workspace) next to the name, such as MYQUIZ (WORKSPACE).

Untitled Multi-Root Workspaces

If you have created a .code-workspace file, then you have already created a second folder to a workspace. Visual Studio Code automatically generates an untitled .code-workspace file for you that contains all the folder settings from your current session. It will remain "untitled" until you save it to the disk.

Now let's talk about workspace and its settings.

Workspace – It is just a collection of folders that will show in the sidebar. They are instrumental whenever you want to group different projects, and then you can have fast access to them from the sidebar.

Creation of Workspace

Let's create our workspace. Go to File > Add folder to Workspace> Select the folder, two folders one by one, and then save your workspace to another location. Whenever you open the workspace saved file, it just shows the collection of paths to our folder like below:

```
{
  "folders": [
  {
   "path": "my-first-app"
  },
```

```
  {
    "path": "my-second-app"
  }
  ]
}
```

How to Perform Searches in Workspace?

When you add some data in the search bar, it will search text from both the folders, such as folder my-first-app and my-second-app separately; you can open files that contain your text.

How Does Source Code Work Inside a Workspace?

When you enable your GitHub source control in the workspace, the inside folder has a separate column of source control, and the changes are tracked separately for project a and project b.

How to Track Your Project in VS Code Workspace Using Git?

Whenever you make any changes in any project, the changes will be tracked by the version control.

What Happens When You Make Changes in Your Working Workspace?

When you change something in your workspace setting, like changing the autosave setting, close the Workspace Settings. These changes will automatically be added to your saved original workspace file.

Open your original workspace for both projects the output will be like this:

```
{
  "folders": [
   {
    "path": "my-first-app"
   },
   {
    "path": "my-second-app"
   }
  ],
    "settings":{
      "files.autoSaveDelay": 1000
      }
}
```

The folder path remains the same, and the settings are added for the autosave delay. In addition to this, the autosave workspace has various attributes like font size, font family, etc.

Search across Files

Visual Studio Code allows you to search over all the files in the currently opened folder quickly. By simply typing "workbench.View.Search" and type in your search. Search results will be shown as grouped files. You can quickly expand a file to see a preview of all the hits within those files. A single click on any file hit will open it in the editor.

Note: We can also use regular expressions while searching in the search box. Let's discuss some familiar terms used for searching in the workspace.

- * – It is used to match one or more characters in the path segment.

- ? – It is used to compare one character in the path segment.

- ** – It is used to match any number of path segments, including none.

- {} – It is used to group conditions example {**/*.html, this syntax will help us to match all the HTML files}.

- [] – It is used to declare a range of characters to match, for example, [0–9].

File Encoding Support

Set the file encoding or workspace by using the "files.Encoding" setting in user settings or workspace settings (Figure 3.3).

You can view encoding in the status bar as UTF-8.

File and Folder Icons

Installation: ext install file-icons

In windows: Go to File > Preference > File Icons Theme > File Icons.

In macOS: Go to Code > Preference > File Icons Theme > File Icons.

Icon Fonts

- File-Icons

- FontAwesome

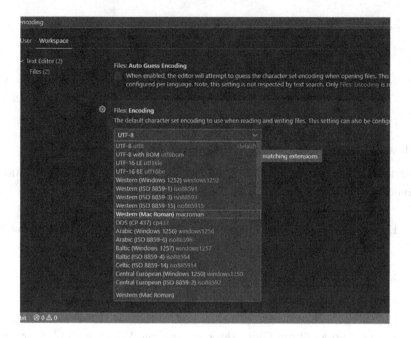

FIGURE 3.3 File encoding settings.

- Mizz

- Devices

- Options

Quick File Navigation

File exploring is great for navigating between files when you are exploring a project. It provides two powerful commands to navigate in and across files with easy-to-use key bindings. Hold Ctrl and press Tab to view a list of all files open in an editor group. To open any of these files, use Tab again to pick the files you want. You can open any files when you type Ctrl + P.

FILES

How to Open Multiple Files in VS Code

First, edit the VS Code settings to enable the support of multiple files at once. To do that, follow the instructions below:

1. Launch VS Code, and then click "File" at the upper part of the program window.

2. Select "Preferences".

3. Select "Settings".

4. Click "Workspace Settings" and locate the "workbench.editor.showT abs". { "workbench.editor.showTabs": true }. If the value is set at "False" change it to "True".

How to Open Multiple Files with Tabs in Visual Studio Code

By default, each new file in VS Code should open in a new tab. Here's how to do that:

1. Launch VS Code and press the Ctrl + P keys at the same time to search for a file to open in the current project.

2. Type in the file name.

3. To open the new file in a temporary tab, click on it once.

How to Open Multiple Files Editor in Separate Windows in VS Code

1. Launch VS Code and press the Ctrl + P keys at the same time to search for a file to open in the current project.

2. By using the "Cmd" key to split your current editor into two or more windows. You can also separate out terminals such as PowerShell, command prompt, Git bash, JavaScript debugging terminal (Figure 3.4).

3. Click on "Split Editor" located at the top right corner of windows to split the current active files into multiple editors.

FIGURE 3.4   Splitting the editor screen.

How to Create New Files and Files Inside a Folder?

Creating new files using VS Code file explorer, you can use a slash in the file name to put the new file inside a specific directory, for example, if you want to make new HTML inside the templates folder, you can do that easily. When you hit the explorer button on the activity bar, the sidebar will be shown right after that. In the sidebar, there are four icons:

- The first icon is used to create a new file.

- The second icon is used to create a new folder.

- The third icon is used to refresh your explorer.

- The fourth icon is used to collapse the folder in explorer.

So click the first icon, enter your folder name, then slash (/) as a representation of your file like templates/home.html, and then hit Enter; it will make templates a directory and home.html as an HTML file.

FOLDER

What Are Development Folders?

Before using your code editor, it's essential to know and understand an organized file system.

Most developers store their projects in an easy-to-find directory (folder). We recommend you call this a directory project. It holds all of your coding projects. Whenever you create a new project, it does not matter how small it is, you always make a new folder inside your projects directory. You will find that single-file projects can turn into large, multi-folder projects.

PROJECT

Project in VS Code

Some users may have grown used to integrated development environments (IDEs) and might have a few problems setting up VS Code to their liking. The next sections explain how to use VS Code to create new projects and manage existing ones.

How to Create a New Project

VS Code does not use the "File > New Project" method which IDEs commonly use to start developing new projects. VS Code is designed to be used as a code editor, which uses your file system to browse existing files in order to edit and compile them.

There is a way to create new projects in VS Code. You need to download a suitable extension from the VS Code Marketplace. An extension will have additional features, but you need to locate a proper debugger with a scaffolder to suit your specific programming needs. Different programming languages and projects require separate extensions to provide a range of functionality, from creating projects to debugging the code.

How to Make a New C# Project in VS Code

To make a new C# project (.NET application), you need to set up scaffolding for your project by configuring the correct prerequisites and then use VS Code to make the new folders.

- Download a C# extension from VS Code Marketspace and install it on VS Code.

- Here's the link to the C-sharp extension of VS Code Marketplace:

- https://marketplace.visualstudio.com/items?itemName=ms-dotnet-tools.csharp

- Download and install a .NET SDK latest version.

- Download as per your system requirements when selecting the download file. It comes in three types: .NET (simple and recommended), .NET (Core), and .NET (Framework).

- Start VS Code in your system.

- Select "File > Open Folder" or in macOS "File > Open" from the VS Code main menu bar.

- In the selection dialog box, create a new folder; rename it according to your project, then click "Select Folder" ("Open" same as in macOS).

- Open VS Code terminal (command prompt) by selecting "View", then click on "Terminal".

- **Enter the following command:** "dotnet new console" in the terminal. This template will create an application with a similar name as the folder.

- VS Code opens a simple program that uses the namespace of your choosing. Then, you can go on and add more functionality to your schedule.

- You have to save changes to VS Code before the program can run. File changes are not saved when you run your program.

- Use the command "dotnet run" to run the program after saving.

That's all. With a C# extension, you can create new folders and create new projects using the command prompt.

How to Create a New Python Project

Python is one of the most popular programming languages, and VS Code has extensions that make programming in Python so easy. Here's what you need to do:

- Install the official Python extension. Here's the link to the Python extension of VS Code Marketplace: https://marketplace.visualstudio. com/items?itemName=ms-python.python

- Use a Python interpreter based on your operating system. For Windows users, it should be python.org, for macOS users should be Homebrew (use the command "brew install python3"). In contrast, Linux users already have built-in integrated Python and only need to use get-pip to obtain more functions.

- Use a terminal to determine and check whether Python has been properly installed or not. The command line "python3 –version" works on macOS/Linux, while Windows needs "py -3 –version" instead.

- Create an empty folder and give the name of your project.

- Use VS Code to open the folder through "File > Open Folder" from the main menu bar.

- Now, configure the Python interpreter with the "Python: Select Interpreter" command in VS Code.

- In the file explorer view (after you have opened your folder with VS Code), create a new file (use the "New File" button) with the same name as the folder and an extension ".py" (this will tell VS Code that it is a Python file).

- Edit your source code if needed and save the result.

- Use the "Run" command on the top of the editor to run the program or by running the command Python file_name.py in the terminal.

PROJECT MANAGEMENT IN VS CODE

To manage a project, you will need the Project Manager for Java extension in VS Code. The extension manages classpaths, packages, classes, and dependencies and creates new projects. The Project Manager for Java extension is included in the Extension Pack, which has other tools for Java development.

Project View

It helps you view your project and its dependencies and provides entry points for project management tasks. You can easily switch between a hierarchy view and a flat view.

Create a Project

You can create a source or project only by clicking the + (plus) sign on project view or by using a command such as Java: Create Java Project. During creation, VS Code facilitates installing the required extension per your project if the extension was not installed.

Import a Project or Module in Java Project

A project is imported to a workspace through the File > Open Folder or the File > Open Workspace menu. For Java will detect your project automatically. You can run the command Java: Import Java projects in the workspace.

Add a Dependency inthe Project

You can add a dependency for the project by clicking the + sign next to the Current Dependencies node in the project view.

How to Add and Export JAR Files

JAR file(s) can be added by clicking the + sign next to Referenced Libraries node in the project view, and you can export your project to JAR from the project view or by running the command Java: Export Jar.

Configure Java Development Kit

Commonly, developers work with various versions of the Java Development Kit. To correctly configure the Java environment and project, you should know two configurations:

1. java.configuration.runtimes

2. java.home.

To configure the JDK you have to run the Java Runtime Configuration wizard. You can run the wizard by opening the Command Palette (Ctrl + Shift +P) and typing the Java: Configure Java Runtime, which brings up the configuration user interface.

JDK for Creating Projects

VS Code detects the runtime required for your project and chooses the suitable configuration from

```
Java.configuration.runtimes
.


\
```

Lightweight Mode in VS Code

VS Code supports two modes of Java, which are:

1. lightweight

2. standard

In the lightweight mode, only source files and JDK are set by the language server. In the standard method, imported dependencies are set, and the project is built by the language server. The lightweight mode works best when you need a super quick-to-start and lightweight environment to work with your source files. For example, reading source code, navigating with source code and JDK, fixing syntax errors, viewing outline and Javadoc, and code completion are supported within the scope of source files and JDK. The lightweight mode does not import dependencies nor build the project, so it does not support running, refactoring, Linting, detecting, debugbing, and amending semantic errors.

You can control modes by configuring "java.server.launchMode" with the below options.

Mode	Description
Hybrid (default)	A workspace is opened with lightweight mode. You will be asked whether to switch to standard mode. Click the server mode on the status bar to switch to normal mode manually.
Standard	A workspace is opened with standard mode.
Lightweight	A workspace is opened with lightweight mode. You can click the server mode icon on the status bar to manually switch to standard mode.

HOW TO BUILD A NEW PROJECT FROM GIT

GitHub is the most popular way to share your work across the world. VS Code allows for a Git integration and easy access to your code by following these steps:

- Download the Python extension.

- Create a new account or log into GitHub.

- Install Git on your local device.

- Open VS Code, then go to "File", then "Settings".

- Type "Git: Enabled" in the search bar of user settings.

- Check the checkbox to ensure Git is integrated with VS Code.

- Create a new repository on GitHub.

- Copy the URL of your repository.

- Open the Command Palette (Ctrl + Shift + P) and type in "Git: Clone <url>" and <url> is the repository URL you just copied.

- You will get a confirmation prompt to clone the GitHub account.

- Click on "Open" when asked to open the new folder, or you can use the "File > Open Folder" dialog.

- Set up a .gitignore file in your project.

- Use a "New File" button on the manager, then type in all the file names if you don't want to commit to GitHub.

- Save the changes.

- Go to the File, then "Save workspace as" to save the project in the folder as a workspace for easier access after.

- To save your VS Code folder to GitHub, use the Checkmark icon to save your changes to the master branch. You can comment to let users know of the differences between the previous and current commit versions.

- Select the dots (three) icon in the corner of the control panel, then select "Push" to push to GitHub.

Now, you are ready to start coding in VS Code and commit changes to GitHub using the Git command.

How Do I Create a New Branch?

To build a new branch for Git projects, follow these steps:

- Click on the icon (branch) in the bottom left corner.

- Once the new branch is created, you need to save it.

- Then switch to the control window (Ctrl + Shift + G).

- Click on the icon (ellipsis) and press "Publish Branch".

- This will publish your newly created branch on GitHub.

CHAPTER SUMMARY

We have learned how to create, manage, edit, and delete files, folders, and projects in this chapter. Also, we learned how to create a project in Python, GitHub, and C++ languages. The steps are similar, but you need to install a different extension from the marketplace because every language requires a unique extension so that VS Code knows that this file is of a particular language.

CHAPTER 4

Editing Code in Your Language

IN THIS CHAPTER

➢ Basic edit of language with useful shortcuts

➢ Programming languages identifiers

➢ JavaScript

➢ Java

➢ C++

➢ Python

➢ CSS, Less, SCSS

➢ TypeScript

➢ PowerShell

In the previous chapter, we covered working with files, folders, and projects in VS Code.

In this chapter, we will learn how to setup the environment of various programming languages for development in VS code.

DOI: 10.1201/9781003311973-4

BASIC EDITING OF LANGUAGE

Before getting deeper into editing code in any language, you should know basic editing in the file using the keyboard and mouse. Visual Studio Code is an editor first and includes the features you need for highly productive source code. This section will take you through the basics of the editor and help you to become more adept with coding.

Keyboard Shortcuts

There are various key shortcuts available in VS Code. VS Code has a rich set of default packages of keyboard shortcuts and allows you to customize them.

1. **Keyboard shortcuts references:** You can get help from VS Code Help > Keyboard Shortcut Reference, which displays a condensed PDF version for easy reference.

2. **Keymap extension:** Keyboard shortcuts play a vital role in productivity and changing keyboarding. For help with the keymap extension, Go to File > Preferences > Keymap. These extensions modify the Visual Studio Code shortcuts, so you do not need to learn new keyboard shortcuts. There is also a keymaps category of extension in the Marketplace.

   There are various popular extensions in the Marketplace. For example:

   - Vim

   - Atom

   - Atom Keymap

   - Bracket Keymap

3. **Customize Keyboard Shortcuts:** Change the default keyboard shortcuts to fit your style.

Adding Multi-Cursor Using the Mouse

You can create additional cursors in a file using the mouse. This lets you select the specific locations where you would like to add cursors. To add cursors to multiple locations, you need to first place your cursor in the desired location and then hold the Alt button on Windows and Linux or options on Mac and click in the locations where you want to add other cursors. You can use multiple cursors to modify various sites in the files. If you don't like using the Alt option for multiple cursors, there are settings that let you change keyboard bindsings via the "workspace" "editor. multiCursorModifier": "alt" to "editor.multiCursorModifier": "ctrlCmd".

Default Key Binding

Key	Command	Command ID
Ctrl + Shift + Alt + Down	Column Select Down	cursorColumnSelectDown
Ctrl + Shift + Alt + Up	Column Select Up	cursorColumnSelectUp
Ctrl + Shift + Alt + Left	Column Select Left	cursorColumnSelectLeft
Ctrl + Shift + Alt + Right	Column Select Right	cursorColumnSelectRight
Ctrl + Shift + Alt + Page Down	Column Select Page Down	cursorColumnSelectPageDown
Ctrl + Shift + Alt + Page Up	Column Select Page Up	cursorColumnSelectPageUp

You can edit keybinding.json to bind them to something more familiar.

Find and Replace

Visual Studio Code allows you to find and replace text in the currently opened file. Press Ctrl + F to open the Find widget in the editor. Search results will be highlighted in the editor. If there is more than one result in the opened file, you can press "Enter" and "Shift + Enter" to navigate to the next or previous result.

EDITING CODE IN YOUR LANGUAGE

Now we are going to talk about programming languages supported by VS Code. Hundreds of programming languages are supported by the Visual Studio Code editor, such as Typescript, HTML, CSS, and JavaScript. More famous languages like Python, C#, PHP, Ruby, Dart, and Go can be used just by installing them from the VS Code Marketplace.

Go to the Marketplace and search for your desired programming language with snippets, code completion/IntelliSense provider, debugger, linter, and more.

Language Documentation

Learn about the programming language supported by VS Code. C++, C#, CSS, Go.HTML, Java, JavaScript, JSON, Julia, Less, PHP, Python,

TypeScript, and Dart. You can learn about these languages in VS Code official documentation.

Some language features in VS Code:

- Syntax highlighting

- Bracket matching

- Intelligent completions, i.e., IntelliSense

- Limiting and corrections

- Code navigation

- Debugging and refractioning

Changing the Language for the Particular Selected File

In Visual Studio Code, the default language support for files is based on their filename extension, for example, .html for HTML, .css for CSS files, and so on. But sometimes, you may want to change the language mode. To do this, simply click on the language indication, which is located at the bottom of the right hand side on the status bar. Whenever we click on this language selector, it will bring up the Select Language Mode dropdown to select another language for the currently active file (Figure 4.1).

The dropdown menu will be like that shown in Figure 4.2.

Keyboard Shortcuts: Ctrl + KM (you will get the same dropdown by running this Change Language Mode).

LANGUAGE IDENTIFIER

Visual Studio Code has a language model with a specific language identifier so that various VS Code features can be enabled based on the current language mode. It is often a lowercased programming language name but not always. You can see the installed languages and their identifiers in the Change Language Mode (Ctrl+ KM) dropdown. VS Code will treat newly created files as plain text.

Spaces: 2   UTF-8   CRLF   HTML   ⚲ Go Live

FIGURE 4.1   Language selecting mode in VS Code.

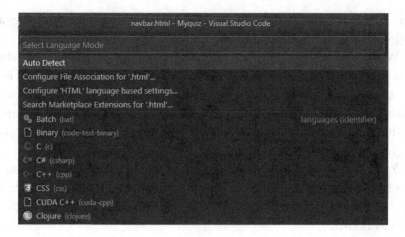

FIGURE 4.2   Select Language Mode dropdown options for selecting a different language.

We can simply identify the new language by using the following guidelines:

- It uses the lowercased programming language name.

- Search for other extensions in the Marketplace to find out if an identifier has already been used.

Here is a list of language identifiers reference:

Language	Identifier
ABAP	ABAP
C	c
C#	CSharp
CSS	CSS
HTML	HTML
Go	go
Diff	diff
JSON	JSON
PHP	PHP
PERL	Perl and perl6
Objective -C	objective-c
SCSS	scss (syntax using curly brackets { }), sass (indented syntax)
Visual Basic	vb
YAML	YAML

You can change the default language settings for files in user settings as follows:

While you are using the "files.defaultLanguage":" in the setting, what you have to do is enter a language identifier as above. If you entered HTML in that space, this would look like "files.defaultLanguage": "HTML", and when you make a new file, this will automatically open as HTML files with manually typing its extension after creating a file. This will help you highlight your content as you make it.

You can also assign a default language model to new files just by adding ${activeEditorLangauge} in the space. It works, as suppose you have opened the HTML and hit Ctrl + N: the new file will have the same extension as HTML.

Adding a Files Extension to a Language

You can also add new file extension to a currently existing language with the "files.association" setting. For example, the setting below adds the .myphp file extension to the PHP language identifier:

```
"files.associations": {
  "*.myphp": "php"
}
```

Let's talk briefly about languages in Visual Studio Code.

JAVASCRIPT

JavaScript in VS Code performs some of the most valuable features like IntelliSense, debugging, formatting, code navigation, and many other advanced features. In IntelliSense, when you write something (app.), this will bring more options by the side like below (Figure 4.3).

This will show you all the methods available for an object, so when we start typing or something else, this will show that something you have typed is a method on our app. This will also show some parameter overloading, so this works for JavaScript, and with typescript out of the box, if you want to add this to other languages, you can install an extension.

Most of the features work out of the box, while some require basic configuration to get a better experience. This section will provide you with knowledge of JavaScript in VS Code. By installing the extension form, the VS Code Marketplace can change most of these built-in features.

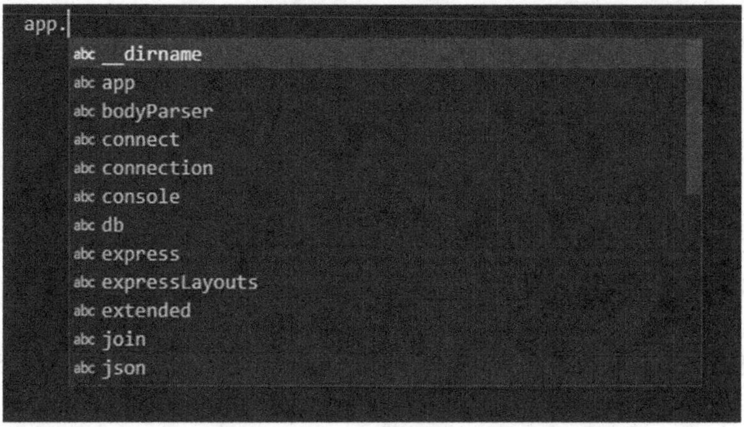

FIGURE 4.3   JavaScript language in Visual Studio Code.

VS Code provides IntelliSense within your JavaScript project for many npm libraries such as React, lodash, and express and other platforms such as node, serverless, or IoT.

WORKING WITH JAVASCRIPT

JavaScript Projects (jsconfig.json)

A file jsconfig.json defines a JavaScript project in VS Code. jsconfig.json is not always required; you need to create one in such cases:

- If all of the JavaScript files in your project workspace should be considered part of a single JavaScript project, this file lets you exclude some files from showing up in IntelliSense.

- Suppose your workplace has more than one project context, such as a front-end and back-end JavaScript code. For the multi-project workspace, you need to create a jsconfig.json at the root folder of each project.

- If you are working on the TypeScript compiler to down-level, compile JavaScript source code.

- Ensure that a subset of JavaScript files in your workspace is handled as a single project. This is very useful if you work with legacy code that uses implicit global dependencies instead of import for dependencies.

To define a basic JavaScript project, add a jscofig.json at the root of your workspace:

```
{
  "compilerOptions": {
  "module": "commonjs",
  "target": "es6"
  },
  "exclude": ["node_modules"]
}
```

Location of jsconfig.json

To define our code as a JavaScript project, create jsconfig.json at the root JavaScript code. A JavaScript project is the files of the project and should not include the derived or packaged files. In more complex tasks of JavaScript, you may have more than one jscongif.json file inside your workspace.

Figure 4.4 shows a project with a client and server folder for two separate JavaScript projects.

Write jsconfig.json

The file jsconfig.json defines the JavaScript target to be ES6 and excludes attributes that exclude the node_modules folder. You can copy and paste this into this file.

```
{
  "compilerOptions": {
  "module": "commonjs",
  "target": "es6"
  },
  "exclude": ["node_modules", "**/node_modules/*"]
}
```

FIGURE 4.4   Jsconfig file for two different project folders.

Exclude attributes tells the languages service which files are not part of your source code. If IntelliSense is working slowly, add the folder to your exclude list. VS Code prompts you to do this if it detects slow completions.

You can set the files in your project using include attribute. If no included attribute is present, this defaults to having all the files in the containing folder and subfolders. When an included attribute is specified, only those files will be included.

For example,

```
{
  "compilerOptions": {
  "module": "commonjs",
  "target": "es6"
  },
  "include": ["src/**/*"]
}
```

Note that file paths in exclude and include are relative to the location of jsconfig.json.

Snippets

Code snippets make it easier to enter repeating code patterns. In VS Code, snippets appear in IntelliSense (Ctrl + Space) mixed with other suggestions. There is also support for tab completion. Enable it with "editor. tabCompletion": "on", type a snippet prefix, and press Tab to a particular snippet.

Built-In Snippets

VS Code has some built-in snippets for several languages: PHP, TypeScript, JavaScript, and Markdown. You can see the present snippets for a speech by running the Insert Snippet command in the palette.

Here is an example of built-in snippets with various options (Figure 4.5).

Install Snippets from the Marketplace

Many extensions in the VS Code Marketplace include snippets. You can simply search for extensions of those snippets in the Extension view (Ctrl + Shift + X) using the @ category: "snippets" filter (Figure 4.6).

Many extensions provide extra snippets, including for most popular frameworks such as Angular, React, or Redux.

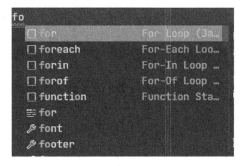

FIGURE 4.5 For loop snippets of JavaScript.

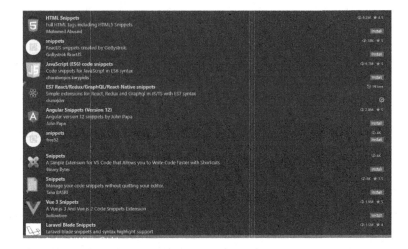

FIGURE 4.6 Snippets extension for various languages.

JSDoc Support

VS Code understands many standard JSDoc annotations and uses these to provide rich IntelliSense. You can use the type documentation from JSDoc comments to type "Check for JavaScript".

Type Checking

It is a great way to catch programming errors or mistakes. It checks to enable some exciting quick fixes for JavaScript, including Add missing and Add missing property. To create JSDoc comments for functions, type "/**" before the function declaration and select the JSDoc comment snippet suggestion.

```
/**Hit enter */
This will show you result like,

/**
 * Add your text in between /** */
 */
```

Hovering Information

Hover over a JavaScript symbol to see its information quickly. By hovering on the function (req, res) of JavaScript files, you will get:

```
(local function) (req: Request<{
id: string;
    }, any, any, qs.ParsedQs, Record<string,
any>>, res: Response<any, Record<string, any>,
number>): Promise<void>
function(req,res)
```

This will give you some brief information about the parameter of the function. The keyboard shortcut Ctrl + K Ctrl + I shows this hover information at the current cursor position.

Signature Help

On the other hand, by using signature help VS Code shows information about the function signature and highlights the parameters that you are currently completing:

```
get(path: "/edit/:id", ...handlers:
RequestHa+ndler<{ id: string; }, any, any,
qs.ParsedQs, Record<string, any>>[]): Router
function(req,res)
```

Auto Imports

Automatic imports are used to speed up the coding suggestion variable throughout your project and its dependencies. When you select one of these suggestions, VS Code automatically adds an import to the top of the files. It will show where they are importing from. For example, in React, we can import various components to make them useful.

```
import React from 'react';
import ReactDOM from 'react-dom';
import App from './App';
ReactDOM.render(
  <React.StrictMode>
  <App />
  </React.StrictMode>,
  document.getElementById('root')
);
```

In React, if you would like to add another component, then VS Code adds an import. In this example, VS Code adds an import for ReactDom from "react-dom" to the top of the file.

Formatting

Visual Studio Code's built-in JavaScript formatter provides basic code formatting with some reasonable defaulst. The javascript. format settings configure the built-in formatter. Or if the built-in formatting is getting in the way, set the "javascript.format.enable" to false to disable it. Install one JavaScript formatting extension like Formatting Toggle, Formatting Essentials, etc.

JSX and Auto-Closing Tags

All of VS Code JavaScript features also work with JXS. So what is JSX? It is a syntax extension to JavaScript. It is used to describe what the user interface looks like. JSX uses the full power of JavaScript. You can use JSX syntax in both .js and .jsx files. It also includes JSX-specific features such as auto-closing of JSX tags. Set "javascript.autoClosingTags" to False to disable tags closing.

```
In HTML,
"html.autoClosingTags": true
In JavaScript,
"javascript.autoClosingTags": true
In TypeScript,
"typescript.autoClosingTags": true
```

Code Navigation

It will let you quickly navigate JavaScript projects:

1. **Go to definitions (F12 or Go > Go to definitions):** It goes to the symbol definition source code.

2. **Peek definition (Alt + F12):** It brings a peek window that shows the definition of the symbol.

3. **Go to reference (Shift + F12):** It shows all the references to a symbol.

4. Go to Symbol in File (Ctrl + Shift + O).

5. Go to Symbol in Workspace (Ctrl + T).

Rename

Press F2 to rename the selected symbol across your JavaScript project.

Refactoring

VS Code includes some good handy refactoring for JavaScript, such as Extract function and Extract constant. Just select what source code you would like to extract and then click on the lightbulb in the gutter or press (Ctrl + .).

Organize Imports

- The organized imports source actions sort the import in JavaScript files and remove any unused imports. You can use the keyboard shortcut Shift + Alt+ O. It can also be done via a user setting.

  "editor.codeActionsOnSave": {}, make it true.

Code Actions on Save

The editor.codeActionOnSave settings let you configure a set of Code Actions that are run when a file is saved. For example, you can enable organize imports on saving by setting:

```
// On save, run both fixAll and organizeImports
source actions
"editor.codeActionsOnSave": {
 "source.fixAll": true,
 "source.organizeImports": true,
}
```

Here are some source actions:

- **"organzieImports"**: It enables organize import on save.

- **"fixAll"**: It auto-fixes on saving and computes all possible fixes in one round.

- **"fixAll.eslint"**: It auto-fixes only for ESlint.

- **"addMissingImports"**: It adds all missing imports on save.

Code Suggestions

Visual Studio Code suggests some common code simplifications, such as converting a chain of .then calls on a promise to use async and await. Set "javascript.sugesstionActions.enabled" to False to disable suggestions.

Update Import on File Move

When you move or rename the file that is imported by other files in the JavaScript project, it can automatically update all import paths that reference the moved file. The "javascript.updateImportOnFileMove.enabled" setting controls this behavior.

- **"prompt"**: It asks if the path should be updated for each file move.

- **"always"**: It always updates paths automatically.

- **"never"**: It does not update the path automatically and does not prompt.

Linters

It provides a warning for suspicious-looking codes. Although VS Code does not include a built-in JavaScipt linter, many JavaScript linter extensions are available in the Marketplace.

For example:

- ESLint

- jshint

- Flow Language Support

- standard – JavaScript Standard Style

Debugging

VS Code comes with great debugging support for JavaScript: inspect objects, navigate the call stack and breakpoints, and execute code in the Debug Console.

Debugging is a built-in feature of Visual Studio Code. It helps accelerate your editing, compilation, and debugging loop.

Debugger Extensions

VS Code has debugging support for the Node.js runtime and can debug JavaScript, TypeScript, or any other language translated to JavaScript. Many debugging languages look for the debugger in the VS Code Marketplace or select install Additional Debugger in the top-level Run menu. Several popular extensions, which include debugging support, are as follows:

- Python

- C/C++

- #

- Debugger for Java

HTML

VS Code provides essential support for HTML (HyperText Markup Language) programming out of the box. There is syntax highlighting, intelligent completion with IntelliSense, and customizable formatting. It also includes Emmet support.

How IntelliSense Works in HTML?

In Figure 4.7 you can see the HTML element closure <div> and a context-specific list of suggested elements (Figure 4.7).

Document symbols are available for HTML, allowing you to navigate to DOM (Document Object Model) node by id and class name.

You can also work by embedding CSS and JavaScript. You can trigger more suggestions by pressing Ctrl +Space.

You can also control whether built-in code providers are active. Override your user and workspace settings with "html.autoClosingTags": true, "html.completion.attributeDefaultValue": "doublequotes", "html .format.enable": true, and so on.

FIGURE 4.7   IntelliSense in HTML language.

Close Tags

Tags elements are automatically closed when > of the opening tags is typed. You can get the tag instantly by typing <div> and then hitting Enter. This will complete your </div> tag.

Auto-Update Tags

When we modify a tag, the linked feature automatically updates the matching closing tag. This feature is optional and can be enabled by setting:

"editor.linkedEditing": true

Hovering

Drag the mouse over the HTML tags or embedded styles and JavaScript to get more information on the symbols under the cursor.

```
Sets the background color of an element.
Syntax: <color>
<button></button>
```

When you move the cursor over the style attribute background, the above line-like sets the background color of an element and displays as long as your mouse is over the attribute.

Formatting

To improve the formatting of your HTML files source code, you should use the Format Document command (Shift + Alt + F) to format the entire file or Format Selection (Ctrl+ K Ctrl + F)

HTML formatted is based on js-beautify – these formatting options are offered by that library.

- **HTML.format.wrapLineLenght:** It allows maximum amount of characters per line.

- **HTML.format.wrapLineLenght:** It is a list of tags that should not be reformatted.

- **HTML.format.contentUnformatted:** It lists comma-separated tags where the content should not be reformatted.

- **HTML.format.wrapAttributes:** Wrapping strategy for attributes:

  1. **auto:** It wraps when the length of the line is exceeded.

  2. **force:** It wraps all the attributes, except first.

  3. **force-aligned:** It wraps all attributes except first.

  4. **force-expand-multiline:** It wraps all attributes.

  5. **aligned-multi:** It wraps when the line is exceeded vertically.

  6. **preserve:** It is preserve wrapping of attributes.

Emmet Snippets

VS Code supports Emmet snippet extension. It is a plugin for popular code editors, which greatly improves HTML and CSS workflow. Here are some features of Emmet snippets:

- Dynamic snippets

- Ultra-fast coding

- Customizable

- Platform for new tools

- Highly portable

```
<!--When you type
ul>li*3>span>
--- Then hit enter the result will be like this-->
<ul>
  <li><span></span></li>
  <li><span></span></li>
  <li><span></span></li>
</ul>
```

HTML Custom Data

You can expand VS Code. The HTML supports the custom data format. In VS Code, there are two methods of loading HTML datasets:

1. With setting HTML.customData

2. With an extension, the provides contributes.html.customData

Both will describe the shape of JSON files. By setting these files, you can enhance VS C'de's understanding of HTML and attribute values.

HTML Extensions

Install an extension to add more functionality to your code. Go to the Extension view (Ctrl + Shift + X), then type HTML to see a list of relevant extensions for creating and editing HTML files. Some of the wings are:

- HTML CSS Support

- HTML Snippets

- IntelliSense for CSS class name in HTML

- HTML Hint

JAVA

Supporting Java in Visual Studio Code provides a wide range of extensions with the combination of the power of core VS Code. These extensions will give you a lightweight code editor that supports many of those common Java development methods.

Visual Studio Code provides essential features such as code completion, refactoring, formatting, code snippets, and unit testing supports. It integrates with tooling and frameworks such as Sprint Boot, Tomcat, etc. This way, a Java developer gets an excellent tool for quick editing, debugging, and testing cycle.

Installation of Java in VS Code

Use the Coding Pack for Java; this is the bundle of VS Code and the (JDK) Java Development Kit. The Coding Pack can also be used to fix a present development environment. The Coding Pack for Java is available for Windows and macOS. For that, you need to install a JDK and Java extension. There are some helpful extension packs for Java:

- Language Support For Java by Red Hat

- Java Test Runner

- Maven for Java

- Visual Studio IntelliCode

- Debugger for Java

There are other popular Java extensions you can pick from as per your needs:

- Spring Boot Tools

- Spring Boot Dashboard

- Jetty

- Tomcat

- CheckStyle

- SonarLint

- Server Connector

You can search for more Java extensions easily using VS Code Marketplace (Figure 4.8).

Before starting anything, check your system has Java SD development (JDK) in your local environment. Once you have installed the Extension Pack for Java, you can open VS Code and experience Java. Open the Command Palette (Ctrl + Shift + P) and type "Java: Getting Started".

Working with Java Source Files

Visual Studio Code supports two Java modes, lightweight and standard. The lightweight mode deals with scenarios that work with the source files, while the standard mode is required only if you want to work with a full-scale project. You can switch between both modes easily.

VS Code Workspaces

Workspaces mean a collection of one or more file system folders and all the VS Code configurations. There are two kinds of "Workspace" in VS Code: "folder workspace" and "multi-root workspace".

A folder workspace is defined when you open a file system folder in VS Code, and "multi-root workspace" can refer to multiple folders from

FIGURE 4.8   Java extension in VS Code Marketplace.

different parts of the file system, and VS Code displays the content of the folder of the workspace together in the File Explorer of the activity bar.

Java Project in VS Code

With IDEs such as Netbeans, IntelliJ, or Eclipse, the concept of "Java" is provided entirely by the extensions but is not a core concept in the base VS Code. When working with "Java projects" in Visual Studio Code, you must have the required extensions installed to work with those project files. For example, Gradle and Eclipse Java projects are supported through Language Support for Java.

Features of language support for Java:

1. As you as types reporting of parsing and compilation errors

2. Type search

3. Call hierarchy

4. Semantic selection

5. Standalone Java files support

6. Code completion

7. Code lens

8. Code navigations

9. Code outline

10. Code snippets

11. Highlights

12. Code formatting

13. Organize imports

VS Code Work Contains Java Project

This section provides you with an overview of how to manage your Java project in VS Code. Managing the project in VS Code requires the Project manager for Java extension. This extension will help drive the classpaths and dependencies and create new projects, packages, and classes. The extension includes the Extension Packs for Java, which also has other tools for development in VS Code.

Project View

The project view helps you view your project and its dependencies and provides entry for your project management tasks (Figure 4.9).

Code Navigation

Java in VS Code also supports source code navigation features such as searching for symbols. Go to the definition and Peek Definitions. The extension Spring Boot Tools extension provides enhanced navigation and code completion support for the Spring Boot projects.

The main advantage of VS Code is speed. You can open your Java project in a few seconds. With the help of lightweight mode, you can navigate your code with the Outline view. This is good to know when you are opening your project for the first time.

Code Completion

IntelliSense is generally used in every language, having code completions and various variable suggestions across all your files. It also provides

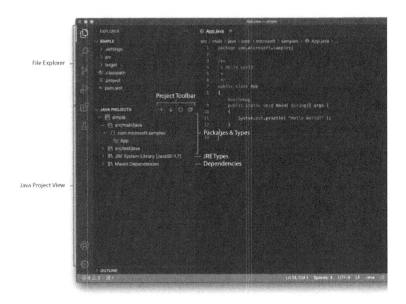

FIGURE 4.9   Java project view.

AI-assisted IntelliSense called IntelliCode. VS Code supports a range of Refactoring and line features.

Debugging

The debugger is a lightweight Java Debugger based on a Java debug server. It works with languages supported by Java, allowing users to debug Java Code within Visual Studio Code. Click on the Run | Debug button or press F5. The debugger will generate the proper configuration automatically for you.

It is lightweight; the Java debugger supports advanced features such as expression evaluation and conditional breakpoints.

Testing

With support from the Java Test Runner extensions, you can quickly run, debug, and manage your JUnit and TextNG test cases. The extension supports the following test frameworks:

- JUnit 4

- JUnit 5

- TestNG

- Requirements

    o JDK (version 11 or later)

    o VS Code

    o Debugger for Java

    o Language support for Java

- Features

    o **Run/Debug:** The extension will generate shortcuts on the left side of the class and method definition.

    o **Test Explorer:** It shows all the test cases in your workspace. You can also run /debug your text case from there.

    o **Customize test configurations:** You can add this configuration into the workspace setting: java. Test.config.

    o **View test results:** After the test cases, the state of the related test items will update both editor decoration and the test Explorer.

    o **VS Code testing commands:** Other testing commands can be found by searching for Test in the Command Palette (Ctrl + Shift + P).

The settings are,

	Description	Default Value Setting Name
Java. test.config	It specifies the configuration for the test cases to run with	{}
Java.test.defaultConfig	It specifies the name of the default test configuration.	" "

C++

Its support for Visual Studio Code is provided by Microsoft C/C++ extension to enable cross-platform C and C++ development on Windows, Linux, and macOS.

Firstly, install the extension.

1. Open Visual Studio Code.

2. Select the Extensions to view on the activity bar or use the keyboard shortcut Ctrl + Shift + X.

3. Select for C++.

4. Select Install.

After installing the extension, you will have high syntax highlighting, intelligent completions, and hover and error checking when you open and file or create a new file.

Install a Compiler

C++ is a compiled language meaning your program source code must be compiled before running on your computer. The C++ extension does not have a C++compiler or debugger. Your work development environment may already provide a C++ compiler and debugger. Some platforms, like Linux or macOS, have a C++ compiler installed. Ensure your compiler is executable in your platform path (%PATH on windows, $PATH on Linux, and macOS). You can even check the availability of your C++ tools by opening the terminal (Ctrl + `) in VS Code.

How to check compiler GCC compiler g++:

g++ version

How to check compiler GCC compiler clang:

clang –version

Install MinGW

Add the path to the Mingw-w64 bin folder for the Window environment PATH variable using the following steps:

- In the search bar, type "settings" to open windows settings.

- Search for the Edit environment variable for an account.

- Choose the Path instance and then select Edit.

- Select New and add the Mingw-w64 se destination folder path, with \ mingw64\bin appended to the system path. The same paths depend on which version of Mingw-w64 you have installed and where you installed it; add this to the path.

- Select Ok to save the updated PATH, and then you need to reopen the console windows t the PATH location.

Write the First Program in VS Code

To make sure that the compiler is installed and configured correctly, we need to create a basic Hello World program.

Create a folder called the first program, and inside, it makes an open file with extension .cpp. For example,

```cpp
#include <iostream>
int main()
{
    std::cout << "Hello World" << std::endl;
}
```

Now press Ctrl + S to save the files. You can enable autosave to save automatically. Run this program by typing "./helloworld". If everything is running perfectly, you will get the output "Hello World".

Debug C++ in VS Code

VS Code supports the following debugger for C/C++ depending on the operating system you are using:

- **Linux:** GDB

- **macOS:** LLDB or GDB

- **Windows:** the VS Code windows debugger or GDB.

Conditional Breakpoints

It enables you to break execution on a particular code line only when the condition's value is true. To set a breakpoint, right-click on a present breakpoint and select Edit breakpoint.

Function Breakpoints

It enables you to break the execution of the function instead of on a code. To set function breakpoint, on the Run view, right click the Breakpoints sections, then choose Add Function Breakpoint.

Expression Evaluation

VS Code supports expression in several contexts:

- You can type an expression into the section of the Run view, and then it will be evaluated each time a breakpoint is hit.

- You can type an expression into debug console, and it will be evaluated at once.

- You can evaluate any expression that appears in your code.

JSON

It is a data format standard in configuration files like project.json or package.json, and its extension should be .json. It is extensively used in Visual Studio Code for our configuration files.

```
{
  "name": "nodejs",
  "version": "1.0.0",
  "description": "rest-full",
  "main": "index.js",
  "scripts": {
   "test": "echo \"Error: no test specified\" && exit 1"
  },
  "keywords": [
   "rest",
   "full"
  ],
}
```

IntelliSence and Validation

You can use JSON data for properties and values with or without schema, and suggestions are offered as you type with IntelliSense. You can manually see the suggestion with the trigger Suggestions command (shortcut: Ctrl +Space). We can perform the structural and value verification based on a JSON schema.

PYTHON

Working with the Python language in Visual Studio Code, using the Python extension, is simple, fun, and productive. This extension makes VS Code editor a more excellent Python editor and works on any operating system with various Python interpreters. It holds all of VS Code's power to provide autocomplete and IntelliSense, debugging, and unit testing, Linting, along with the ability to quickly switch between Python environments, including virtual and Conda environments.

This provides only an overview of the different capabilities of the Python extension for VS Code.

Installation of Python and the Python Extension

This part of this chapter guides you through installing Python and using the extension. Firstly, you have to install a Python interpreter yourself separately from the extension in your local system. Use Python from python .org (its official site) for a quick install and install the extension from the VS Code Marketplace.

Once you have installed Python, activate it using the Python: Select Interpreter command. You can even set this manually.

Run Python Code

To get experience in Python, create a new file and call it myfirstprogram.py, and copy/paste ("HELLO PYTHON") into it. The Python extension gives you the shortcuts to run Python code in the selected interpreter.

Ways to Run Python Program

In the text editor, right-click anywhere in the editor and select Run Python File in the terminal.

In explorer, just right-click the Python file and select Run Python File in the terminal.

You can use the Terminal: Create New terminal command to create a terminal in VS Code that automatically activates the currently selected interpreter. The Python: Start REPL lets you activate the terminal with the presently selected interpreter and then runs the Python REPL.

Autocomplete and IntelliSense

Python supports code completion and IntelliSense using the interpreter. It is a general term for several features, including impressive IntelliSense code completion of all your files and built-in and third-party modules.

It quickly shows method and class methods as you start typing, and it can trigger completions at any time with Ctrl + Space. By hovering over the text, you get more information about them.

CSS, SCSS, AND LESS

VS Code has built-in support for editing and modifying the CSS (cascading style sheet) sheet, with the extensions .css, .scss, and .less. You can also install an extension for improved functionality:

- SCSS IntelliSense

- Stylelint

- HTML CSS Support

- Beautify css/sass/scss/less

Syntax Coloring and Preview

As you start typing, the syntax is highlighted in the context preview of colors. On clicking a color preview, an integrated color picker is launched, which supports configurations like opacity, saturation, and hue.

You can also hide the Visual Studio Code color preview by inputting the following setting:

```
"editor.colorDecorator": false
```

To disable CSS, Less, and SCSS, use the following command in user settings:

```
"[css]":{
        "editor.colorDecorators" :false
}
```

Folding

You can fold regions of code using the following icons on the gutter between line number s and line start. Folding parts are available for all decorators.

Additionally you can use the following region markers to define a folding region: /"#region"/ and /#endregion*/ in CSS/SCSS/Less or //region and //#endregiond in SCSS/Less.

```
"[css]":{
        "editor.foldingStrategy" :"indentation"
}
```

Emmet Snippets

Emmet snippets are built into VS Code, and suggestions and other offers and snippets in the editor auto-completion list are listed below.

Emmet abbreviations and snippets expansions are expanded by default in pug, HTML, slim, jsx, XML, CSS, Scss, Sass, style, and stylus files as any language that takes over from above like handlebars and PHP.

When you start writing an Emmet abbreviation, you will see the built-in abbreviation displayed on the right side of the suggestion list. If you are in an HTML file, when you start typing tag <, you will instantly get the entire tags suggestion list. See the example in Figure 4.10.

If you are working on a style sheet file, the abbreviation in the suggestion list is sorted with the other CSS suggestions (Figure 4.11).

Using Tab Key for Emmet Expansions

If you like to use the Tab key for expanding the Emmet abbreviations of any file, add the following settings:

"emmet.triggerExpansionOnTab": true

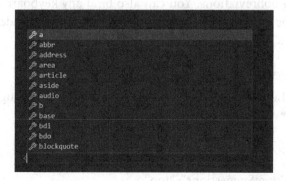

FIGURE 4.10   Emmet abbreviation of tags in HTML file.

FIGURE 4.11   CSS Emmet abbreviations in CSS file.

This will allow using the Tab key for indentation when text is not an Emmet abbreviation.

Emmet Abbreviations When quickSuggestions Are Disabled

If you disabled the editor.quickSuggestions option in the settings, then you won't see any suggestions as you type. You can trigger suggestions manually by pressing Ctrl + Space.

How to Disable Emmet Abbreviations in Suggestions?

If you do not want to see the Emmet abbreviations in the suggestions at all, then you can change the setting:

"emmet.showExpandedAbbreviation": "never"

If you want, you can use the command Emmet: Expand Abbreviation to expand your abbreviations. You can also bind any keyboard shortcut by changing the settings of workspace "emmet.showExpandedAbbrevia-tion": "always".

Emmet Suggested an Ordering List

To use this, Emmet suggestions always come on top of the suggestion list; add the following settings in the workspace:

"emmet.showSuggestionsAsSnippets": true,

"editor.snippetSuggestions": "top".

To enable Emmet abbreviation expansion in file types where it is not available by default, use the emmet.includeLanguages setting.

```
"emmet.includeLanguages": {
 "javascript": "javascriptreact",
 "razor": "html",
 "plaintext": "pug"
}
```

Make sure you use language identifiers for both sides of the mapping, with the right side being the language identifier of an Emmet-supported language.

Emmet does not know any new languages, so there might be Emmet suggestions showing up in non HTML/CSS contexts. To keep away from this, you can use the following setting.

"emmet.showExpandedAbbreviation": "inMarkupAndStylesheetFilesOnly"

Use of Filter

Filters modify the expanded abbreviation before it is output to the editor. There are two ways to use filters:

1. Either globally through the emmet.syntaxProfiles setting

2. Directly in the current abbreviation

Below is an example of the first approach using the emmet.syntaxProfiles setting to apply the abc filter for all the abbreviations in HTML files:

```
"emmet.syntaxProfiles": {
 "html": {
  "filters": "abc"
 }
}
```

Comment Filter in Snippets

The filter will add comments around essential tags. By default, "important tags" are those tags with id and class attributes.

For example div>div#page>p.title+p|c will be expanded as:

```
<div>
 <div id="page">
 <p class="title"></p>
 <!-- /.title -->
 <p></p>
 </div>
 <!-- /#page -->
</div>
```

HTML has custom snippets that apply to all other markup types like the pug templating engine. When its value is an abbreviation and not actual HTML, the appropriate transformations can get the correct output as per the language type.

For example, for an unordered list <ul> with a list item <li>, if your snippet value is ul>li, you can use the similar snippet in pug, html, haml, but When you snippet value is <ul><li></li></ul>, then it will work only in html files.

If you would like a snippet for plain text, then surround the text with {}.

CSS Emmet snippets should be a property name and value pair. Its custom snippets apply to whole other style sheets like SCSS, Less, or Sass. CSS Emmet will add it as needed based on whether the language requires it. The snippet name should be separate property name and value.

Install Sass and Less into CSS

This code editor can integrate with Sass and Fewer transpilers through the task runner. We use this to transpile .scss or .less files into .css files. Let go with transpiling a simple Sass/Less file.

1. Install a Sass or Less transpiler.

If you do not have Node.js and the npm package manager installed in your system, you will need to install it. Install Node.js for your local platform. The Node Package Manager is included in the Node.js distribution.

```
C:\Users\PC> npm install -g sass less
```

The output will be like this:

```
Debugger listening on ws://127.0.0.1:56594/58be
59d8-1e8a-4fd8-a453-7678be195b40          e195b40
```

```
For help, see: https://nodejs.org/en/docs/inspector
Debugger attached.

added 35 packages, and audited 36 packages in the 20s

One package is looking for funding
  run `npm fund` for details

found 0 vulnerabilities
Waiting for the debugger to disconnect...
```

CSS, SCSS, and Less Settings Configuration

You can configure the following warnings as User > CSS and Workspace > CSS (search CSS in search bar) Settings. This setting allows you to turn off the built-in validation.

Id	Description	Default
less.validate	Enables or disables all less validations	true
css.validate	Enables or disables all CSS validations	true
scss.validate	Enables or disables all SCSS validations	true

To configure for CSS, use CSS.lint as the prefix to the id for SCSS or less use as similar scss.lint and less.lint.

Lint checks are performed as you type the following:

Id	Default	Description
validate	true	Enables or disables all validations.
compatibleVendorPrefixes	ignore	Use when a property with a vendor-specific prefix, make sure also to include all other vendor-specific properties.
boxModel	ignore	You do not use width or height when using padding or border.
universalSelector	ignore	It warns when using the universal selector * as it is known to be slow and should be avoided.
important	ignore	It warns an indication that the specificity of the entire CSS has gotten out of control and needs to be refactored.
float	ignore	Using float as floats lead to fragile CSS that is easy to break if one aspect of the layout changes.
idSelector	ignore	It warns when using selectors for an id #id as selectors should not contain IDs because these rules are too tightly coupled with the HTML.

TYPESCRIPT

JavaScript was first introduced for the client-side language. As its code grows, it tends to get messier, making it difficult to maintain and reuse. Its failure to hold Object Orientation features, strong type checking, and compile-time error checks prevent JavaScript, but typescript works as a bridge for these languages.

TypeScript is JavaScript for application-scale development. It is a compiled language, strongly typed and object-oriented. It was designed by Anders Hejlsberg. It is a superset that complies with plain JavaScript. It offers you classes, modules, and interfaces that help you to build robust components.

Install the TypeScript compiler

Visual Studio Code's editor includes TypeScript language support but doesn't include the TypeScript compiler. You will need to have installed the TypeScript compiler either globally or in your workspace to transpile TypeScript source code into JavaScript.

The east way to install TypeScript is through npm, the Node.js Package Manager,

Npm install –g typescript or npm install – save-dev typescript to check the version by, tsc - - version.

Syntax and Semantic Highlighting in TypeScript

TypeScript and JavaScript also provide syntax highlighting as well as semantic highlighting.

1. Syntax highlighting colors the text based on lexical rules, and semantic highlighting enriches the syntax coloring based on resolved symbols.

2. Semantic highlighting is visible depending on the current color theme. Each theme can configure whether to display semantic highlighting.

3. When semantic highlighting is enabled, and the color theme has a corresponding styling rule defined, different colors and styles can be seen, and semantic highlighting can change colors based on some parameters,

Semantic highlighting can change colors based on:

- It resolved the type of a symbol like a namespace, variable, property, variable, property, class, interface, type parameter.

- Whether the variable/property is read-only or modifiable.

- Whether the variable/property type is callable a function type or not

IntelliSense

It shows you the intelligent code completion, hovers info, and signature information so that you can write code more correctly and quickly. It provides IntelliSense for individual TypeScript files as well as TypeScript in the tsconfig.json file of the projects.

Snippets in Visual Studio Code

The Snippets are templates that make it easier to enter repeating code patterns, for example, looping statements or conditional statements. Snippets appear in (Ctrl+ Space) IntelliSense mixed with other suggestions. It also supports tab-completion enabling it with "editor.tabCompletion": "on" or pressing Tab to insert a snippet. It (Snippets) follows the TextMate snippet syntax.

How to Install Snippets from the Marketplace

VS Code Marketplace includes many snippet extensions. You can search for extensions containing snippets in the Extensions view (Ctrl+ Shift + X) using the @category: "snippets" filter.

If you find an extension and install it, then restart VS Code, and the new snippets will be available right after.

Custom Snippets

You can define your snippets without the need for an extension. To create or edit your snippets, select User Snippets under File > Preferences in windows or mac, code> Preferences on macOS, and then select the language for which the snippets should appear. This code editor manages the creation and refreshing of the underlying snippets file(s) for you.

Snippets files are almost always written in JSON, and support C-style comments can also define an unlimited number of snippets. Snippets can support most Text Mate syntax for the intelligent format, dynamic behavior, whitespace based on the insertion context, and easy multiline editing.

Below is an example of a print to console snippet for CSS.

```
"Print to console": {
 "prefix": "log",
 "body": [
 "console.log('$1');",
 "$2"
 ],
 "description": "Log output to console"
 }
```

There are various attributes in the code

1. **Prefix:** It can be defined as one or more trigger words that display the snippet in IntelliSense.

2. **Body:** It is more than one line of content, which is joined as multiple lines upon insertion. New lines and embedded tabs will be formatted according to the context in which the snippet is inserted.

3. **Description:** It is an optional description of the snippet displayed by IntelliSense.

Snippet Scope in Typescript

These are scoped so that only relevant snippets are suggested. Either can scope snippets:

- the language snippets scope
- the project snippets scope

Let's discuss snippets scope one by one. So first is language snippet scope.
    Every snippet is scoped to one or all languages, and it is defined in two files:

1. a language file

2. a global file

Single-language custom-defined snippets are defined in a specific language snippet file (for example, css.json), which you can access by language identifier through Preferences > Configure User Snippets. It is only accessible when editing the language for which it is defined.

Multi-language or custom-defined snippets are defined as "global" snippet files, which can also be accessible through Preferences > Configure User Snippets. A snippet definition may have an additional scope property that takes one or more languages as identifiers which makes the snippet available for specified languages. Most of the user-defined snippets are scoped to a single language.

Snippet syntax snippets can use particular constructs to control cursors with the text being inserted. The following are features and their syntaxes:

- Tabstops

- Placeholders

- Choice

- Variables

Hovering Information

It is hovering over a JavaScript symbol to see its information quickly. By hovering the Main function () of TypeScript files, you will get:

```
                function thingParts(): string
function Mainfunction() {
  return "My Super Important thing has this parts:"
}
```

This will give you some information about the parameter of the function. The keyboard shortcut is Ctrl + K Ctrl + I, which shows this hover information at the current cursor position.

Auto Imports

Automatic imports are used to speed up the coding suggestion variable throughout your project and its dependencies. When you select one of these suggestions, VS Code automatically adds an import to the top of the files.

You can disable auto import in settings "typescript.suggest.autoImport": false.

Formatting

Visual Studio Code built-in Typescript formatter provides basic code formatting with some reasonable default. The TypeScript. format settings configure the built-in formatter. Or, if the built-in formatting is getting in the way, set the "typescript.format.enable" to false to disable it. For specialized coding formatting styles, install one of the Typescript formatting extensions like Formatting Toggle, Formatting Essentials, etc.

JSX and auto-closing tags

All of VS Code JavaScript features also work with JXS. So what is JSX? It is a syntax extension to JavaScript. It is used to describe what the user interface looks like. JSX is coming with the full power of JavaScript. You can use JSX syntax in both .js and .jsx files. It also includes JSX-specific features such as auto-closing of JSX tags. Set ""typescript.autoClosingTags": true" to false to disable tags closing.

```
In TypeScript,
"typescript.autoClosingTags": true
```

Code Navigation

It will let you quickly navigate JavaScript projects.

1. Go to definitions (F12 or Go > Go to definitions) – The source code of symbol definition.

2. Peek Definition (Alt + F12) – It brings a peek window that shows the definition of the symbol.

3. Go to reference (Shift + F12) – It shows all the references to a symbol.

4. Go to Symbol in File (Ctrl + Shift + O).

5. Go to Symbol in Workspace (Ctrl + T).

Refactoring

VS Code includes some good handy refactoring for JavaScript, such as Extract function and Extract constant. Just select what source code you like to extract and then click on the light bulb in the gutter or press (Ctrl +.)

TypeScript refactoring includes:

1. **Extract to method or function:** It extracts the selected statement or expressions.

2. **Extract to constant:** It extracts the selected to a new constant in the files.

3. **Extract type to interface:** It extracts the selected complex type.

4. **Move to the new file:** It moves or more classes, functions, constants, or interface in the top-level scope to the new file.

5. **Convert between named imports and namespace import:** It converts between named imports.

6. **Convert get and set assessors:** It encapsulates a selected class property by generating a getter and setter for it.

7. **Convert parameter to destructed object:** It rewrites function that takes a list of arguments to take a single argument object.

TYPESCRIPT'S UNUSED VARIABLES AND UNREACHABLE CODE

New TypeScript code is an unreferenced import; sometimes we initialize some variables but do not use them in our code so that TypeScript can highlight that variable, and when we right-click on that, it shows the message of unused variable.

To disable the new code, set "editor.showUnused" to false in the setting.

```
"[typescript]": {
  "editor.showUnused": false
},
"[typescriptreact]": {
  "editor.showUnused": false
},
```

Organize Imports

The organized imports source actions sort the import in a typescript file and remove any unused imports. You can use keyboard shortcuts Shift + Alt+ O. It can also be done by a User setting.

"editor.codeActionsOnSave": {}, make it true.

Code Actions on Save

The editor.codeActionOnSave settings let you configure a set of Code Actions that are run when a file is saved. For example, you can enable organize imports on saving by settings:

```
// On save, run both fixAll and organizeImports
source actions
"editor.codeActionsOnSave": {
  "source.fixAll": true,
  "source.organizeImports": true,
}
```

Here are some source actions:

- **"organzieImports"**: It enables organize import on save.

- **"fixAll"**: It auto fix on saving computes all possible fixes in one round.

- **"fixAll.eslint"**: It auto-fix only for ESlint.

- **"addMissingImports"**: It adds all missing imports on save.

Code Suggestions

Visual Studio Code suggests some common code simplifications, such as converting a chain of .then calls on a promise to use async and await. Set "typescript.sugesstionActions.enabled" to false to disable suggestions.

POWERSHELL

It is a task-based command-line shell, scripting language built on .NET, which provides you a powerful toolset for administrators on any platform.

The PowerShell extension has rich language support and capabilities such as completions, definition tracking, and Linting analysis for PowerShell.

Installation of the PowerShell Extension

The official PowerShell extension can be installed by following the Visual Studio Code User Guide steps or by going directly to the Visual Studio Code Marketplace and clicking the Install Button.

You can also install the PowerShell extension from within Visual Studio Code by opening the Extensions view with keyboard shortcut Ctrl + Shift + X and typing "PowerShell", and selecting the PowerShell extension.

Install from the Command Line

The PowerShell extension can be installed from any of the command lines such as PowerShell, bash, Command prompt on all the platforms using the following command:

Code – install-extension ms-code.Powershell

And for VS code insider, then the command will be:

Code-insider – install-extension ms-vs code.Powershell

Major Features of PowerShell

1. It provides Syntax highlighting.

2. It provides code snippets from making coding easy.

3. Provide IntelliSense for cmdlets and more.

4. The rule-based analysis provided by PowerShell ScriptAnalyzer.

5. "Go to definition" of cmdlets and variables.

6. Provide find references of cmdlets and variables.

7. Document and Workspace symbol discovery.

8. Run selected section of PowerShell code using F8.

9. Launch online help for the symbol under the cursor using Ctrl + F1.

10. Local script debugging and basic interactive console support.

11. Enable ISE mode using Ctrl + Shift + P, then search for "Enable ISE Mode".

PowerShell Extension Settings

You can change the Visual Studio Code setting from the file> Preferences >Settings menu item (Code > Preferences > Settings on macOS). Also, you can use the keyboard shortcut Ctrl +, top open user settings. The VS Code has introduced a setting GUI in version 1.27.1 as the default interface for customizing settings.

You can easily open the settings.json file using the Preferences: Open Setting (JSON) command from the Command Palette or by changing the default setting with the workbench.settings.editor setting.

Multi-Version Support

You can change the PowerShell extension to use any version of PowerShell installed on your local machine by following these steps:

1. Open the Command Palette on Windows or Linux with Ctrl + Shift + P. On macOS, use Cmd + Shift + P.

2. Search for Session.

3. **Click on PowerShell:** Show Session Menu.

4. Choose the version of PowerShell you want to use from the list.

You can also change the version by clicking on the version in the right corner of the screen or running the PowerShell: Show Session Menu command from the Command Palette (Ctrl + Shift + P).

CHAPTER SUMMARY

In this chapter, we have learned about VS Code languages support like HTML, Python, PowerShell, TypeScript, JavaScript, C++, JSON, etc. We also learned about topics like IntelliSense, debugging, validations, snippets, extensions, filter, hovering information, auto import, and formatting in each section so that you can efficiently work on these languages.

CHAPTER 5

Integrating with Source Control

IN THIS CHAPTER

➢ Git source control

➢ SCM (source control management)

➢ SVN (subversion control)

In the previous chapter, we learned how to set up the environment of various programming languages for development in VS Code like HTML, Python, PowerShell, TypeScript, JavaScript, C++, JSON, etc. and also covered topics like IntelliSense, debugging, validations, snippets, extensions, filter, hovering information, and so on. In this chapter, we will talk about integrating source control using Git, SCM, and SVN.

USING VERSION CONTROL IN VISUAL STUDIO CODE

VS Code has integrated source control management (SCM). Visual Studio Code provides you with so many built-in extensions, for example:

- SVN

- Git Extension Pack

- Hg

- Perforce for VS Code

DOI: 10.1201/9781003311973-5

TYPES OF VERSION CONTROL

- **Local version control Systems:** It is the most common VCS with the simplest form and has a database that keeps all the changes to files under revision control.

- **Centralized version control systems:** This type of version control systems contains only one repository, and each user gets their working copy.

  The following are required to make your VCS:

  o You commit

  o They update

- **Distributed version control systems:** This type of version control system contains multiple repositories. Each repository has its repository and working copy.

  The following are required to make your VCS:

  o You commit

  o You push

  o They pull

  o They update

PURPOSE OF VERSION CONTROL

- Multiple people can work simultaneously on a single project.

- It enables a single person to use multiple computers to work on a project.

- It provides access to the historical versions of a project.

Many organizations and developers either use a centralized version control system (CVCS) like subversion (SVN) or Distributed Version Control systems (DVCS) like Git (Written in C) and so on.

USE OF VERSION CONTROL SYSTEM

- **A repository:** It can be thought of as changes in the database. It contains all the edit snapshots of the project.

- **Copy of work:** It is the personal copy of all the files in a project. You can edit this copy without affecting the work of others.

INTEGRATION WITH GIT SOURCE CONTROL

Visual Studio Code is a well-known editor to support various development activities and programming languages. You can learn briefly about VS Code in Chapter 1. But here, we are going to talk about Git in VS Code.

Git is a source control platform. It helps you to manage the development activities. It notes down the status of your project every time any change happens.

VISUAL STUDIO CODE AND GIT SOURCE CONTROL

Visual Studio Code integrated Git source control. It supports other various source controls such as SCM, TFS, and Azure Repos using extensions. Its options are – Open Folder and Clone repository (Figure 5.1).

We can open a repository folder or clone from a GitHub URL. But here, we will clone the repository from GitHub in the VS Code. Firstly, you should log in to your GitHub profile, view its files, and copy the repository URL (Figure 5.2).

In the VS Code, click on the cloned repository. If it asks for GitHub URL, paste the URL and click on the clone from the URL. You get a prompt while it clones the repository from the GitHub URL you specified.

Once the cloning process is complete, the prompt window pops up on your screen, asking: Would you like to open the cloned repository?

Click on Open to see all the files in VS Code repository. You can compare the VS Code repository and the GitHub repository.

Git Status Bar Actions

In the status bar, you get the following (Figure 5.3):
In Figure 5.3 the icon is defined as,

- **Branch:** It shows you the Git branch. It uses a master branch for all the scripts and the changes as default.

- **Synchronize:** You should click on Synchronize changes to synchronize the VS Code repository with the upstream branch. It pulls the

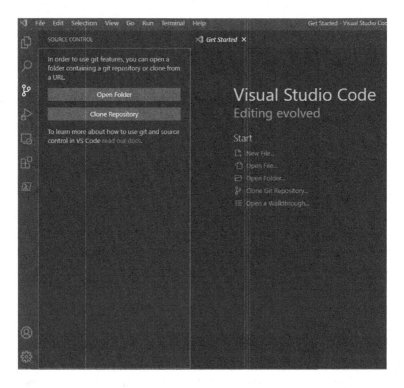

FIGURE 5.1 Git source code.

remote changes down to your local repository and pushes local commits to the upstream branch. The Publish action is enabled if no upstream branch is configured and the Git repository has remote setup.

- **Programming language:** The third will tell you which programming language you are using in your project. In this case, Python is used.

- **Errors and warnings:** If your code contains any kind of errors and warnings, these indicators highlight them.

Gutter Indicators

When you make changes in the Git repository scripts, VS Code adds a few annotations in the gutter. Let's talk about indicators.

- A red triangle is for the deleted line.

- A green bar is for the newly added line.

- A blue bar is for some modification lines.

Sign in to GitHub

Username or email address

|

Password   Forgot password?

Sign in

New to GitHub? Create an account.

Terms   Privacy   Security   Contact GitHub

FIGURE 5.2   GitHub login.

FIGURE 5.3   Git status bar.

Viewing Diffs

It performs the functionality to perform diff queries on files. It compares the changes with the last commit file in a Git repository. You have to download a separate diff tool to do this, so built-in features can help you work more efficiently. To view how it works, open any script in the Git repository and make the changes.

- Few codes are removed after the last commit. It shows in the red background.

- Few codes are unchanged after the last commit. It has no background color for those lines.

- Few codes are removed after the last commit. It shows in the red background.

Diff Editor Review Pane

There is a preview pane in the diff editor that presents changes in a unified patch format. You can navigate between changes with Go to the Next Difference (F7) and Go to Previous Difference (Shift + F7). The lines can be navigated with arrow keys, and pressing Enter will jump back in the diff editor and the selected line.

Timeline View

It is accessible at the bottom of the File Explorer by default. Its built-in Git support provides the Git commits history of the specified file. When you right-click on a commit, you will get options to Copy Commit ID and Copy Commit Message. VS Code supports more Git history workflows through extensions; you can install them from VS Code Marketplace.

- GitLens

- Git history

- Git graph

- Git history diff

Git Output Window

VS Code provides a Git output window that shows you the command. It will help you to learn Git languages and commands.

In the VS Code, go to the Command Palette (Ctrl +Shift + P) -> Git: Show Git Output. It opens an extra window for Git output, and you can see all the commands in real time (Figure 5.4).

Git Extensions

Visual Studio Code provides several extensions to extend the functionality of Git source control. You can also install these git extensions from VS Code Marketplace. Click on Extensions in the menu and search for the Got keyword. It will show you all the related attachments in the list (Figure 5.5).

FIGURE 5.4   Git output window.

FIGURE 5.5   Git extension in VS Code Marketplace.

Git Blame

It gives information about the person who modifies the code in the VS Code status bar. Suppose someone changes the code intentionally. Its purpose is to keep others aware of the changes, and you can ask the developer questions in case any issues occur. This provides the ability to view Git Blame Information in the status bar for the currently selected line.

Working with Branches

Move to the status bar, and you can create and switch branches. If you look at the bottom left of the editor, you should see the source control icon followed most likely by the master or the name of the working branch.

To create a branch, click on the branch name. A pop up shows and gives you the option to create a new branch and then create a new branch called demo. Now, change your file that signifies you are in the new demo branch, such as adding the text this is the latest demo branch.

Commit those changes to the demo branch. Again, click the branch name in the bottom left to switch back to the master branch.

After switching back to the master branch, you will notice that the demo branch is no longer present.

GitLens

It changes the Git capabilities built into Visual Studio Code. It helps you to visualize code authorship at a glance via Git blame annotations and code lens, navigate and explore Git repositories, gain valuable insights via powerful comparison commands, and so more.

This extension is one of the most popular in the community and is also the most powerful. In most ways, it can replace each of the previous two extensions with its functionality.

It is powerful, feature-rich, and highly customizable to meet your needs. It helps you better understand code. Here are some of the features of GitLens.

It also enables effortless revision navigation through the history of the file, authorship code lens, a status bar blame, rich remote providers integrations, many powerful commands for navigating and comparing revision, and user-defined modes for quickly toggling between sets of settings.

Git History

You can view current changes, performs diffs, and manage branches with the built-in features in VS Code, but it does not provide in-depth view into your Git. Also, explore the history of a file, author, and branch; launch it from the VS Code Command Palette. You can get the various options in the command.

- View Git history

- View files history

- View line history

The main features are:

- You can see the difference in the files changes in the gutter.
- The Git status bar shows the current branch, dirty indicator, incoming and outgoing commits.
- You can do most of the things in Git operation from within the editor:

  1. Initialize a repository.

  2. Clone a repository.

  3. Create branches and tags.

  4. Stage and commit changes.

  5. Push/pull/sync with a remote branch.

  6. Resolve merge conflicts.

  7. View diff.

Git Support

It ships the Git SCM extension. Most of the source control user interface and workflow are common across other SCM extensions. The icon on the activity bar on the left side will always indicate an overall how many changes you currently have made in your repository. Selecting the icon shows you the details of your current repository changes such as change, staged changes, and merge changes. By clicking each item will guide you in more information about the textual changes in each file. For unstaged, the editor on the right still helps you to edit the file. Clicking on each item will show you in detail the textual changes within the file.

You can find some indicators of the status of your repository in the bottom left corner of VS Code, such as the current branch, dirty hands, and the number of incoming and outgoing commits of the current branch. You can check out and branch in your repository by just clicking that status.

Commit in GitHub

The Git command is used to move files from the staging level to a commit. This command always runs after the Git adds, which is used to add files to the staging area. Git commit creates a snapshot of the changes made to a Git repository, which can be pushed to the main repository. Staging (using Git add command in Git Bash) and unstaging (using Git reset command in Git Bash) can be done via contextual actions in the files or drag and drop.

You can type a commit message above or use the keyboard shortcut Ctrl + Enter (Windows) and ⌘ + Enter (macOS) to commit them. When there are any staged changes, only those changes will be committed. Otherwise, you will always get a prompt to select what changes you would like to commit.

Note: If you commit your changes to the wrong branch, you can undo your commit using "Git: Undo Last Commit" command in the Command Palette.

Cloning a Repository

If you have not opened it yet, the source control view will give you two options: Open Folder from your local machine or Clone Repository. Local repositories on GitHub are remote repositories. You can even clone or fork a repository with the Github Desktop to create a local repository on your computer. Whenever you clone a repository, you should push any changes to GitHub, affecting the original repository. To make changes without changing the actual projects, you can create a separate copy by forking the repository.

Github Desktop will automatically prompt you to create a fork when you try to use Github Desktop to clone a repository that you don't have write access to. You can choose your fork to contribute to the original upstream repository or work on your project independently. You can change your current choice at any time.

Steps to clone your project:

1. On the menu bar, click on the file, then click "Clone repository".

2. Click the tab that is similar to the location of the repository you are going to clone. You can click any of the options, Github.com, Enterprise, or URL.

3. Choose the repository you want to clone.

4. Click Choose option and navigate to a local path where the repository was cloned.

5. Then click on the clone.

What Is Forking in GitHub?

So, a fork is just a copy of the repository. Forking your repository allows you to experiment with changes without affecting your original project freely.

When you clone a repository that you do not have access to, GitHub will create a fork. After creating or cloning a fork, the Github Desktop will always ask you to use the fork.

Steps to fork your repository:

1. On the menu bar, click on the file, then click Clone repository.

2. Click the tab location of the repository you want to clone. You can click any of the options Github.com, Enterprise, URL.

3. Choose the repository you want to clone from the list.

4. Click Choose and navigate to a local path where you want to clone the repository.

5. Then click on the clone.

6. If you use this fork to contribute to the original upstream repository, click "To contribute to the parent project". They will help you to contribute to the desktop/desktop repository.

7. If you plan to use this fork for a project not connected to the upstream, click For my purposes.

8. Click on Continue.

Git Command Palette

GitLens provides you the customizable Git Command Palette command (gitlens.gitCommands) to provide guided access to many common Git commands with quick access to commit history and search, stashes, and more (Figure 5.6).

Branches and Tags

You can create and check out branches directly within Visual Studio Code editor through the Git: Create Branch and Git: Checkout to commands in the Command Palette (Ctrl + Shift +P).

If you run Git: You will see a dropdown containing all of the branches or tags in the current repository. It will give you the option to create a new branch or to check out a branch or tag in detached mode.

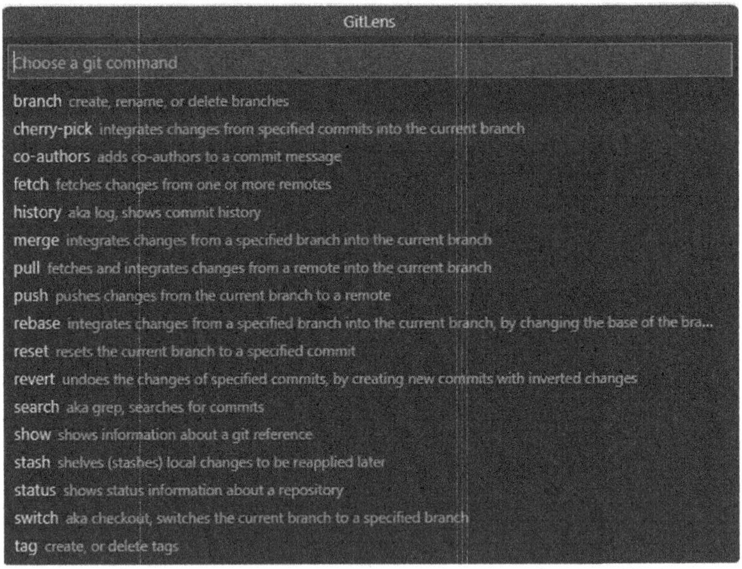

FIGURE 5.6 GitLens provides various extensions.

The Git: It can create branch command that let you quickly create a new branch. Please provide the name of your new branch, and VS Code will create the branch and switch to it.

Remotes in Github

Remote in Git is a common repository that all team members use to exchange their changes in the repository. Visual Studio Code offers some beneficial actions like push, pull, and syncing that branch. You can find actions in the Views section and More Actions... along with the option to add or remove a remote. VS Code can periodically get changes from your remotes. This will enable VS Code to show how many changes your local repository is ahead of. By default, this feature is disabled, and you can use the Git.autofetch settings to enable it.

Working with Remotes

To work with the Git project, you need to know how to manage your remote Git repositories. It is a version of your projects that are hosted on the internet or network somewhere. You can have various repositories, but each one is either read-only or read/write for you. Managing remote repositories requires knowing how to add remote repositories, removing those that are no longer valid, defining them as being tracked or not, and more.

Showing Your Remotes

You can run the Git remote command to see which server you have configured. It lists the name of each remote handle. You can see the origin, that is, the default name Git gives to the server you cloned from. Here is an example of Git cloning of the repository.

```
$ git clone https://github.com/your_respository
Cloning into 'your_respository'...
remote: Reusing existing pack: 1857, done.
remote: Total 1857 (delta 0), reused 0 (delta 0)
Receiving objects: 100% (1857/1857), 374.35 KiB |
268.00 KiB/s, done.
Resolving deltas: 100% (772/772), done.
Checking connectivity... done.
cd your_respository
git remote
origin
```

You can specify –v as that shows you the URLs that Git has stored for the shortname to be used when reading and writing to that remote: Using the "-v " options, you will also see the remote's URL in listings.

```
$ git remote -v
origin https://github.com/ your_respository (fetch)
origin https://github.com/ your_respository (push)
```

Git Remote Add

When we fetch a Git repository implicitly, it adds a remote for the repository. We can add a remote for a repository. You can add a remote as a nickname. To add remote as a short, follow the below command in the Git Bash:

```
$ git remote add <short name><remote URL>
```

Fetching and Pulling Branch

You can easily fetch and pull data from the current repository. The fetch and pull command runs out to the server and fetch all the data from that remote project. The commands let us fetch all the branches from that remote.

```
git fetch <remote_branch>
```

To clone the repository from your remote projects, run the command:

```
$ git clone<remote>
```

The remote repository is added by using the default name "origin". The command is used as Git fetch origin.

The Git fetch command is only for downloading the data to the local repository. You can only add or modify data when you operate the command. To pull the repository, execute the command below.

```
$ git pull <remote>
```

Pushing to Remote Branch

The Git push command can be used to share a project or send an update to the server. It is used as:

```
git push<remote> <branch>
```

To update the central branch of the project, run the command:

```
$ git push master
```

The origin stands for the remote repository, and master is defined as the main branch.

Git Remove Remote

To remove a connection, run the Git remote command with the remove or rm (short form) option as:

```
$ git remote remove < destination>
```

Or

```
$ git remote rm < destination>
```

Git Remote Rename

By using the below command, you can rename your repository name as:

```
$ git remote rename <old name> < new name>
Example
$ git remote rename Project1 Project2
```

Git Show Remote

To see all the information about the specific remote server, use the Git remote command as:

```
$ git remote show <remote>
```

It will show all the information related to the remote server and contains a list of branches related to it.

Git Change Remote

We can change the URL of any remote repository. The Git remote set command is used to change the URL of the repository.

```
$ git remote set-url <remote name> <newURL>
```

The remote set-URL command has two types of parameters. The first one <remote> is about the current server name for the repository. The second argument <new URL> is about the new URL name for the repository.

```
$ git remote -v
$ origin https://github.com/URLChanged (fetch)
$ origin https://github.com/URLChanged (push)
$ git remote set-url <remote name> <newURL>
```

Adding Remote Repositories

Git clone command will add the origin remote implicitly. Here is how to add a new remote explicitly. To add a remote Git repository as short name, run Git remote add <short name> <url>.

```
$ git remote
origin
$ git remote add new_name https://github.com/your_
respository
```

```
$ git remote -v
origin https://github.com/your_respository (fetch)
origin https://github.com/your_respository (push)
new_name https://github.com/your_respository (fetch)
new_name https://github.com/your_respository (push)
```

You can use the string new_name on the command line. For example, if you want to retrieve all of the information in the repository, you can run Git fetch new_name.

```
$ git fetch new_name
remote: Counting objects: 43, done.
remote: Compressing objects: 100% (36/36), done.
remote: Total 43 (delta 10), reused 31 (delta 5)
Unpacking objects: 100% (43/43), done.
From https://github.com/new_name
 * [new branch]  master -> new_name/master
 * [new branch]  your_repository -> new_name/
your_repository
```

Fetching and Pulling from Your Remotes

To get data from your remote project:

```
$ git fetch <remote>
```

The command goes out to that remote project and pulls down all the data from the remote project. After this, you should reference all the branches from that remote, which you can merge or inspect at any time.

If you clone a repository, the command adds the remote repository name "origin" automatically. So Git fetch origin fetches new work that has been pushed to that remote server since last fetched. The Git fetch command only downloads the data to your local repository. You have to merge manually once you are ready.

If your active branch is set up to track a remote branch, you can use the Git pull command to fetch and then merge the branch into the current branch. Then Git clone command is used to set up a local master branch to track the remote master branch. Running the Git pull fetches cloned data from the server and automatically tries to merge it.

Pushing to Your Master

When your project is at the point that you want to share it, you have to push it upstream. The command is very simple: git push <remote> <branch>.

If you push your master branch to your origin server, then you can push my commits.

```
$ git push origin master
```

This command only works when someone clones from a server for which you have write access.

Inspecting a Remote

If you would like to see more information about a particular remote, you can use the Git remote show <remote> command.

```
$ git remote show origin
* remote origin
 Fetch URL: https://github.com/your_repository
 Push URL: https://github.com/your_repository
 HEAD branch: master
 Remote branches:
 master          tracked
 dev-branch          tracked
 Local branch configured for 'git pull':
 master merges with remote master
 Local ref configured for 'git push':
 master pushes to master (up to date)
```

It will show you the entire URL for the remote repository as well as tracking branch information. If you are on the master branch and run Git pull, it will automatically merge the remote master branch. It will merge instantly the master branch into the local one.

If you are using Git more heavily, then you must see more information by using Git remote show:

```
$ git remote show origin
* remote origin
 URL: https://github.com/my-project
 Fetch URL: https://github.com/my-project
 Push URL: https://github.com/my-project
 HEAD branch: master
 Remote branches:
 master          tracked
 dev-branch          tracked
 markdown-strip          tracked
```

```
issue-43    new (next fetch will store in remotes/
origin)
issue-45    new (next fetch will store in remotes/
origin)
refs/remotes/origin/issue-11 stale (use 'git remote
prune' to remove)
Local branches configured for 'git pull':
dev-branch merges with remote dev-branch
master merges with remote master
Local refs configured for 'git push':
dev-branch    pushes to dev-branch    (up to date)
markdown-strip    pushes to markdown-strip    (up to
date)
master    pushes to master    (up to date)
```

This command will show which branch is instantly pushed to when you run Git push while on specific branches. It will also show you the branches on the server you do not have yet, which remote branches you have been removed from, and multiple local branches that can merge instantly with their remote-tracking branch when you run Git pull.

SCM (SOURCE CONTROL MANAGEMENT)

The source control API allows the extension authors to define SCM features. A slim, robust API surface allows various tough SCM systems to be integrated with Visual Studio Code while having a familiar user interface with all of them.

Source code management tools are important when more than one developer is working within a shared area, and it is common to make edits to a shared chunk of code. Many separate developers may be working on a seemingly single feature; however, this feature may use a shared code module. Therefore, Developer A working on Feature 1 could make some edits and find out later that Developer B working on Feature 2 has conflicting edits.

Before using SCM, developers often edited their text files directly and moved them to remote locations using FTP or other protocols.

Developer A would make edits, and Developer B unknowingly saved over Developer A's work and cleaned out the changes. SCM acts as a protection mechanism against this specific scenario; this is known as version control. Source control management brought version control safeguards to prevent loss of work due to overwriting. These work by tracking changes from each developer. This conflict mechanism has the side effect of providing passive communication for the development team.

The Benefits of SCM

The version control SCM provides a suite of other helpful features to make collaborative code development a more user-friendly experience. When SCM has started tracking all the changes to a project over time. The SCM provides valuable record-keeping for a project release version notes. SCM reduces team communication and increases release velocity. Without SCM, the development is slower because contributors have to take extra effort to plan a non-overlapping sequence of action but can work independently on separate branches with developers. CM is a must-have in the modern age of software development.

Features

- Commits are cheap and easy to make in SCM. They frequently capture updates to a codebase. A group of commit commands can be combined into a single commit.

- It enables rapid updates from more than one developer. It is easy to have a local copy of the codebase.

- A commit has a corresponding log entry; this log entry is populated with a message.

- SCM offers a "staging area." The staging can be used to collect a group of edits before writing them to a commit.

- Branching is a powerful mechanism that allows the users to create a different line of development. It should be used frequently as they are quick and inexpensive.

- The staging area is used to manage and review changes before creating the commit snapshot.

- Branches enable multiple developers to work in parallel on separate lines of development. These lines of action are generally different product features.

Source Control Model

Source control is responsible for populating the source control model with instances of "SourceControlResourceState" resource states.

These resource states are themselves organized in groups, for example, "SourceControlResourceGroup".

Create a new source control with "vscode.scm.createSourceControl". The following is the output of Git status

```
vsce main* → git status
On branch main
Your branch is up-to-date with 'origin/main.'
Changes to be committed:
  (use "git reset HEAD <file>..." to unstage)
  modified: README.md
  renamed: src/api.ts -> src/test/api.ts
Changes are not staged for commit:
  (use "git add/rm <file>..." to update what will be
committed)
  (use "git checkout -- <file>..." to discard
changes in the working directory)
  deleted: .travis.yml
  modified: README.md
```

There are many things in this workspace. The first file is the README. md which has been modified, staged, and then changed once again. The second file, the src/api.ts, has been moved to src/test/api.ts, and that move was staged. Finally, the .travis.yml file has been deleted.

This workspace, Git, defines two resource groups:

1. The working tree

2. The index

Each file change within that group is resource state:

- **Index:** resource group

- **README.MD, It modified:** resource the state

- **src/test/api.ts, It renamed from src/api.ts:** resource the state

- **Working tree:** It is known for the resource group

- **.travis.yml, deleted:** It is known for resource state

- **README.md, modified:** It is known for resource state

Source Control View

Visual Studio Code can populate the source control view as the source control model changes. Resource states are customizable using "SourceControlResourceDecorations".

```
export interface SourceControlResourceState {
 readonly decorations?:
SourceControlResourceDecorations;
 }
```

The resource state optionally provides a command to handle this action:

```
export interface SourceControlResourceState {
 readonly command?: Command;
 }
```

Input Box of SCM

This box, located atop each source control view, allows the user to input a message. You can even get and set this message to perform operations further. For example, in Git, this is used to commit the box, in which users type in commit messages and Git commit commands pick them up.

```
export interface SourceControlInputBox {
 value: string;
 }
 export interface SourceControl {
 readonly inputBox: SourceControlInputBox;
 }
```

SVN

SVN stands for subversion. It is a centralized version control system that means a single server contains all files and revisions from those users who can check out any version of any file.

When files are checked out from a remote subversion repository, the user gets a snapshot of the repository. To make use of subversion for your version control, it should be installed on your machine.

To check if subversion is installed on your machine, use the following command in terminal:

```
svn - -version
```

This command will return the version number installed in your machine.

Some graphical user interfaces for subversion (SVN) may also allow the use of your computer's command line to interface with repositories. Still, the recommended Windows client, Tortoise, does not. To use the command line, in some cases, a separate command-line SVN client must be installed. Two such clients are:

1. **external link: Slik:** It provides clients for Windows, Mac, and Linux.

2. **external link: CollabNet:** It is a second option that is a command-line client for Windows only.

When these are installed, you can navigate a DOS or terminal window to a local repository folder.

- **svn info:** It provides information about that folder's, latest updates, current revision, etc.

- **svn update:** It updates the folder to match the current revisions in the repository.

- **svn commit:** It commits recent changes in the local folder to the repository.

Benefits of the Version Control System

1. It enhances the project development speed by providing efficient collaboration.

2. It reduces the possibilities of errors and conflicts.

3. It helps in recovery in case any disaster occurs.

CHAPTER SUMMARY

In this chapter, we have discussed version control systems, i.e., a software tool that helps in recording changes made to files. We also discussed various options for version control systems and we have learned about Git, SCM (source control management), and SVN (subversion control).

CHAPTER 6

Debugging Code

IN THIS CHAPTER

➢ Debugging code

➢ Linter or Linting

➢ JS Lint

In the previous chapter, we talked about integrating source control using Git, SCM, and SVN. Here we will discuss the most important topic, debugging, which is basically used to free your code from warnings and errors. We will also cover some topics like debugging tools, Linting, and JS unit Linting in depth.

One of the critical features of the editor Visual Studio Code is debugging. It has a built-in debugger that helps accelerate your edit, compile, and debugging loop. The below image will show the debugging console where you see various errors and warnings (Figure 6.1).

Figure 6.2 will show the debugging icon in the status bar to see various errors and warnings.

DEBUGGER EXTENSIONS

Visual Studio Code has built-in debugging support for the Node.js runtime and can debug JavaScript, Typescripts, or other languages that get transplied to JavaScript. For debugging other languages (PHP, PowerShell, Ruby, Go, C#, C++, etc.), look for debugger extensions in the VS Code

DOI: 10.1201/9781003311973-6

FIGURE 6.1 Debug console.

FIGURE 6.2 Debug console in the status bar.

Marketplace or select the Install Additional Debuggers in the top-level Run menu.

Here are the various popular extensions which include debugging support:

- Python

- C/C++

- C#

- Debugger for Java

Now let's start with debugging.

It is a core feature of Visual Studio Code. We will see how to run and debug a program in VS Code and explore some debugging features and breakpoints. Here you are going to learn debugging for Node.js. So, firstly you must have Node.js installed on your PC to use this feature.

In Visual Studio Code, debugging is a powerful tool support for Nodej. js runtime, and we can debug JavaScript, TypeScript, and many other languages that were transplied into JavaScript. Setting up a project for Node. js debugging is straightforward, with VS Code providing appropriate configuration default and snippets.

There are a few ways you can debug the Node program in VS Code.

- You can use an auto attach to debug processes you run in VS Code integrated terminal.

- With the use of the JavaScript debug terminal, similar to using the integrated terminal.

- You can use launch config to start your program file or attach it to a process launched outside of Visual Studio Code.

Auto Attach

If the auto attach feature is enabled in the project, the Node debugger automatically attaches to specific Node.js processes launched from VS Code integrated terminal. Use the Toggle Auto Attach command from the command palette (Ctrl + Shift + P) to enable the components if there is already an auto attach icon in the Status bar.

There are various modes for auto attach, which you can select in the result Quick Pick and via the debug.javascript.autoAttachFilter setting:

- **Smart:** If you execute a script outside your node_modules folder, use a standard "runner" script like mocha or ts-node; this process is used for debuggers. You can also configure the runner script, which allows a list using the Auto Attach Smart Pattern setting.

- **Always:** It means that all the Node.js processes launched in the Integrated Terminal will be debugged.

- **onlyWithFlag:** Here, only the process launched with the - - inspector - -inspect-brk flag will be debugged.

When auto attach is enabled, you need to restart your terminal. There will be one icon in the top right of the terminal. You need to click this icon. Then the debugger should connect to your program within a second.

Additional Configuration

Configuration

You can apply other properties to auto attach in the debug.javascript.terminalOptions setting. The entire debugging configuration is stored in the launch.json file located in your workspace .vs code.

The following features are supported in the configuration of launch launch and attach:

- **outFiles:** It is an array of glob patterns for generating JavaScript files.

- **resolveSourceMapLocations:** It is an array of glob patterns for location files.

- **trace:** It enables diagnostic output.

- **skipFIles:** It automatically skips files covered by these glob patterns.

- **remoteRoot:** It tries to automatically step over code that doesn't map to source files.

- **stopOnEntry:** It breaks immediately when the program launches.

- **smartStep:** It tries to automatically step over code that doesn't map to source files.

These attributes are only available for launch configuration of request launch:

- **program:** It is an absolute path to the Node.js program to debug.

- **args:** It is the argument passed to the program to debug. It is of type array and expects individual argument as an array element.

- **cwd:** It launches the program to debug in this directory.

- **runtimeExecutable:** It is an absolute path to the runtime executable to be used.

- **env:** It is an optional environment variable. This will expect the environment variable as a list of the string typed key/value pairs.

- **console:** The console path to a file containing environment variable definitions.

- **runtimeVersion:** If "nvm" or "nvs" is used for managing Node.js versions, these attributes can be used to select a specific version of Node.js.

- **envFile:** It is the optional path to a file containing environment variable definitions.

These attributes are only available for launch configuration of request attach:

- **restart:** It restarts the connection on termination.

- **Port:** It holds debugging port to use.

- **Address:** It is the TCP/IP address of the debug port.

- **processID:** It is the debugger that tries to attach to this process after sending the usr1 signal.

- **Protocol:** It debugs protocol to use.

- **continueAttach:** whether to continue the process if it is paused when we attach to it.

The following are some Node.js snippets:

- **Launch Program:** Launch a Node.js program in debug mode.

- **Launch via npm:** Launch a Node.js program through npm debug scripts. If you have defined npm debug script in your package.js, you can use it directly from your launch config. Make sure that the debug port should use in the npm scripts.

- **Attach:** It is the debug port of a locally running Node.js program. You should make sure your node program to debug has been started in debug mode and the debug port used is the same as the one specified in the snippet.

- **Attach to Remote Program:** It is the port of a Node.js program running on the host specified by the address attribute. The Node program to debug has been started in the debug mode, and the debug port used is the same as the one specified in the snippet.

- **Attach by Process ID:** The process picker is open to select a node or down process for debugging. With this configuration, you can even attach a node or down process that was not started yet in the debug mode.

- **Nodemon Setup:** It regularly uses nodemon to relaunch a debug session whenever the JavaScript source has been changed. Make sure that you have nodemon installed globally in your project or system. Remember that terminating the debug session only stops when the program debugs, not nodemon itself. To terminate nodemon in your project, press Ctrl + C in the Integrated Terminal.

- **Mocha tests:** It debugs mocha tests in a test folder of your project. You should make sure that your project has "mocha" installed in its "node_modules" folder.

- **Yeoman generator:** It is debugging a yeoman generator. The snippet will ask you to specify the name of the generator. Ensure that your project has "yo" installed in its node_modules folder and that your generated project has been installed for debugging by running the npm link in the project folder.

- **Gulp task:** Debug a gulp task that makes sure that your project has "gulp" installed in its node_modules folder.

- **Electron Main:** Debug the primary Node.js process on an Electron application. The snippet is that the Electron executable has been installed inside the node_modules/.bin directory of the workspace.

Node Console

By default, The Node.js debug sessions launch the target in the internal Visual Studio Code Debug Console. The Debug Console does not support programs to read input from the console, and you can enable either an external terminal or use the VS Code Integrated Terminal by setting the console attribute in your launch configuration to externalTerminal or integratedTerminal, respectively. The default is called internalConsole.

When an external terminal is used, you can configure the terminal program to use "terminal.external.windowsExec", "terminal.external.osxExec", and "terminal.external.linuxExec settings".

Launch Its Configuration to Support npm and Other Tools

Instead of using the Node.js program directly with a node, you can use npm (node package manager) scripts or the other task runner tools now from a launch configuration:

- Any program available on the PATH (example, npm, gulp, etc.) can be used for the "runtime executable" attribute and arguments that can be passed via "runtimeArgs".

- You do not need to set the program attribute if your npm script or another tool implicitly specifies the program to launch.

Let's look at an npm example. If your package.json file has a "debug" script, for example:

```
{
  "name": "project",
```

```
"version": "1.0.0",
"description": "Project",
"main": "app.js",
"scripts": {
 "test": "echo \"Error: no test specified\" && exit 1",
 "start": "node app.js"
}
}
```

The above code describes the Node.js package.json file, the first field name tells you the name of the project, the version on which version you are building the project, the description gives the project name, main tells you from which file your project will runs and scripts.

```
"scripts": {
 "test": "echo \"Error: no test specified\" && exit 1",
 "start": "node app.js",
"debug" : "node main.js"
}
```

How to Enable Node.js Debug Mode in VS Code

When you install Visual Studio Code in your system, open your VS code, then run Ctrl + Shift + P to open the Command Palette, or you can open the file in the menu bar then click on the Preferences > Settings and in the search box type "node debug". Look for Debug >Node: Auto Attach. It is set to disable by default. Click it and turn it on. This will enable the Node .js application. You can also look for an Auto Attach: On statement at the blue bottom bar in Visual Studio Code to confirm. Then you will get the desired result (Figure 6.3).

FIGURE 6.3   Node.js debugging in VS Code.

Next, open the Node.js project file you want to debug and set some breakpoints by clicking on the left-hand side of the files where you would like to stop your code and in the terminal type node --inspect <FILE NAME>.

Note: A red dot will appear when a breakpoint has been set. The breakpoint will help you to identify the line or region where your code is falling.

VS Code Debugging in Action

Once you hit Enter, your VS Code terminal turns orange at the bottom to indicate you are in debug mode, and your console will print a message along the lines of "Debugger Attached". Now, you can see some breakpoints in the bottom left corner of the screen, and you can step through the code like little play, step over, step in, restart, etc. buttons at the top center of the IDE. VS Code even highlights the breakpoints and lines you have stopped on with yellow, making it easier to follow along.

As you step forward from breakpoint to breakpoint, you can see the program printing out the console.log in the debug console at the bottom of the VS Code and the yellow highlighting.

Debug with Nodemon

It is a tool that auto-reloads the server and reattaches the debugger after making changes to your project. You can install using npm install node-mon in the terminal. Then add the following configuration in your launch .json.

```
{
  "name": "Attach to node",
  "type": "node",
  "request": "attach",
  "restart": true,
  "port": 9229
}
```

Now you can launch your app normally, replacing node with nodemon. Example: nodemon - - inspect <filename>.

And if you get an error such as nodemon: command not found, it means nodemon was not appropriately installed; then for Windows, use npm install – g - -force nodemon, and in macOS sudo npm install –g - - force nodemon.

Various Options to Debug in Node.js

There are several ways to debug your Node.js program. Here is a list of some of the methods for debugging in Node.js:

- **Console.log():** It is an excellent way to debug your programming errors. It is a function that writes a message to log on to the debugging console. We will not see anything on the screen. It only logs an error to a debugging console. It is built in Node.js and JavaScript in the browser console.

    In Java, we are using the system. Out.println() we can perform debugging in a Java project.

    In Python, using print(), we can perform debugging in a Python project. This is the most straightforward implementation and the fastest way to clean extra lines of information.

- **Node.js documentation - -inspect:** The Node docs themselves understand debugging is not easy, but they made a handy reference to help people out.

- **JetBrains:** It is one of the famous software development companies. IntelliJ and Webstorm are IDEs, but Jetbrains is great. They have a fantastic ecosystem of plug-ins for their tools.

- **Visual Studio Code:** VS Code is all in one, which has every new feature, and it makes users love this IDE.

DEBUGGING TOOLS

What Is Debugging Tool?

With almost as much technology as we use today, challenges like viruses and flaws in our operating system are certain to arise. Fortunately, JavaScript debugging tools are available to help developers combat internal computer bugs by increasing visibility, which includes the ability to take a snapshot of your overall application state. This visibility assists in the early detection of viruses.

Debugging tools, commonly known as debuggers, enable more in-depth analysis and testing. They are always putting a theory of issues to the test and studying the finest feasible future situations. This boost in speed and simplicity when addressing internal issues helps a company or individual to save a significant amount of time and concentrate on the work that the bug would have occupied otherwise.

Dealing with bugs and viruses is becoming increasingly common among programmers' tasks. When you need to solve an issue, you need the correct debugging programs with the necessary tools to assist ease the process. It's important to invest ahead of time and be prepared before the problem arises. You'll save a lot of time and have a lot less discomfort as a result of this.

Today's browsers include a number of web building tools. Most popularly known as add-ons or extensions, these tools are not just only for web development, but also serve a lot of other functions, of which debugging is one of the most well known. These tools make your job effortless and help you in inspecting and analyzing the issues with the CSS, HTML, and JavaScript used in the code. Here, we have listed the top 12 most commonly used browser debugging tools. These will help you debug and inspect your code and inspect the HTTP headers, access various FTP source files, and evaluate the accessibility of the web page.

1. **Firefox Developer Tools:** It is a fantastic set of tools with many features to explore, examine, and debug websites and web pages. You can easily see and modify the page HTML and CSS using this fantastic tool. Apart from that tool, with its inbuilt JavaScript debugger, you can stop anything, step through explorer, and modify the JavaScript running in a file. Storage Inspector tells you about the inspect cookies, local storage, and session storage present on a page.

2. **Chrome Developer Tools:** It is a fixed set of web developer tools inbuilt to Google Chrome. It helps you to edit pages and remove errors in the program code. "The Dev Tools for beginners" is a fantastic tool to learn the fundamentals of web development for the beginner. Explore the tool and then easily view and change a page style, debug JavaScript, and even optimize the website's speed.

3. **Web Developer:** It is an extension for Firefox and a few other browsers that provide you with a toolbar with many options with features for debugging and inspecting web pages. This tool is helpful primarily for working with large CSS files and other projects that you may be unfamiliar with. It has a built-in feature for validating the page's syntax and helps you locate the possible errors.

4. **Safari Developer Tools:** You should ensure your website works well with all the significant web browsers using Safari Developer Tools. It comes equipped with Web Inspector, a powerful tool that simplifies the work of modifying, debugging, and optimizing a website for optimal performance and compatibility on other different platforms. Its responsive design mode helps you get an examination of your web pages for various screen sizes, orientations, and resolutions.

5. **Internet Explorer Web Edge (Developer) Toolbar:** It is the tool for you if you are looking for that that resembles the Firebug in functionality. With this tool, you can easily edit the web page DOM and HTML directly in the web browser. It also lets you change, manage, and edit DOM elements to inspect what happens as you perform predefined actions or modify the code. Besides it, you can use this tool to test and debug JavaScript with the IE Web Developer Toolbar.

6. **Fiddler:** It is an extension of the Internet Explorer browser that lets you debug web applications and analyze web page HTTP traffic. It will help you to set up breakpoints and has a lot of other features useful for debugging. This tool is fully extensible and even lets you create your scripts to perform valuable functions.

7. **Open Dragonfly:** It is a commonly popular web development tool integrated into the web browser Opera. You can detect all the network traffic, edit colors, view the DOM, and debug JavaScript. You just need to download it once in your system, but it can be in offline mode, too. It is a cross-platform operating system developed by Opera Software.

8. **DebugBar:** It is a free tool for personal and educational purposes that helps you debug a program in code. It is an in-browser extension for IE (Internet Explorer). Using this tool, you can send a web page screenshot via email and view both the original and interpreted code. It has a color picker and a Console API. It helps to gain some quick and easy information using a command-line interface.

9. **YSlow:** It is a tool that helps you analyze web pages to understand why they are working slow. It works on Yahoo rules for high-performance websites and displays various relevant statistics on a page. It also gives suggestions for improving the performance of web pages and summarizes the page's components.

10. **HTTPWatch:** It is another traffic viewer and debugger, similar to Fiddler with its working and approach. Features of HTTPWatch are generating request level time charts, decryption of HTTPS traffic to assist debugging, exporting captured data to XML and CSV formats. It offers a free basic edition as well as a professional and advanced edition.

11. **Live HTTP Headers:** It's a Firefox add-on that allows you to examine HTTP requests and response headers. With the aid of this tool, you can debug your web apps by looking at the HTTP headers. Besides that, the tool assists you in obtaining information about a website's server and analyzing cookies given to the client when requesting a specific page.

12. **Venkman JavaScript Debugger:** It is accessible as an add-on and aids in the debugging and troubleshooting of sophisticated JavaScript. The console view provides a command-line interface for interacting with the debugger. When active functions hit the breakpoint, the tool's Stack View feature allows you to step through them.

13. **Rookout:** It is a tool that brings agility to the debugging process. In both servers, it can debug in various programming languages like JVM, Node.js, and Python to code more minor applications. Its beauty lies in its ability to allow users to debug both staging and production applications quickly and securely. It removes the lengthy and complicated debugging processes by providing all the data needed in a matter of seconds. The on-demand data it supplies ensures developers can understand and debug issues within their program's code without coding, redeploying, or restarting their applications.

- **Some Highlights**
  - o Easy to get started
  - o Seamless Git integration
  - o Interaction tracking and screen sharing capabilities
  - o Provides comprehensive debugging data in real time
  - o Integrates with a range of tools, including Slack, Datadog, Sentry, Sumologic, and more

  The tool will give you complete visibility into your app's performance, so you can trace issues and develop appropriate fixes. It makes all this possible without the need to install software on the end-user.

14. **RubyMine:** It is a powerful and intelligent cross-platform IDE that allows debugging Ruby on Rails, Coffee Script, CSS, JavaScript, ERB (Embedded Ruby) and HAML, and much more. Its advanced built-in debugger allows you to set breakpoints and define hit conditions with ease. It is a great tool that will enable you to launch multiple debug processes simultaneously. You can even run your applications on the remote device and then add the Ruby interpreter.

   • **Highlights**

     o It is based on the solid IntelliJ IDEA platform.

     o Good support for ruby-related frameworks and technologies.

     o Autocomplete feature is pretty good.

     o Good Git integration.

     o Supports multiple plugins.

     o Integrates seamlessly with rails.

15. **PyCharm:** It is another robust IDE developed by JetBrains for Python. It is an impressive code editor equipped with remote development capabilities, including running, testing, deploying, debugging, and small hosting applications on virtual machines. The debugger also offers several breakpoints, frames view, watches, stepping modes, remote interpreters, and a debug console. It is a beautiful cross-platform development tool. Other than Python, it supports some languages like JavaScript, CoffeeScript, Python, TypeScript SQL, HTML/CSS, Node.js, AngularJS, and many more.

   • **Some Highlights**

     o Incredible connectivity with various databases for queries within the IDE.

     o Automatic code completion.

       – Searching and installing packages is easy.

     o It shows code errors on the fly and facilitates easy fixing.

     o Git visualization.

16. **Eclipse:** It is an IDE for Java development that supports languages like PHP, Python, Ruby, and C#. It is equipped with advanced features for development and debugging, making it an all-rounder tool and many more.

One of the essential features of Eclipse is the platform debug perspective that shows detailed debugging information such as breakpoints, variables, call stacks, and threads side by side.

Using Eclipse, you can step through program execution, suspend and resume threads, evaluate expressions, and inspect values. Managing remote debugging configurations on Eclipse is relatively straightforward, which makes the tool more popular among developers.

- **Highlights**

    o Automatic code completion

    o Good refactoring support

    o Excellent navigation capability

    o Helps with syntax checking for clean and efficient code

    o Git integration

Debugging Tools Features

The below are some of the most frequent characteristics seen in debuggers:

- Built-in tools

- Dashboards

- Encrypted communication

- Examination of the state of the application

- Code editor

- GIT integration

- Integrates with latest technologies

- Memory protection

- Processes real-time errors

Debugging Tools Comparison

- **Ease of use**. The learning curve for certain debugging software is greater than that for others. It depends on how much time you have or are willing to invest to learn the system; nonetheless, keep ease of use in mind before making a purchase.

- **Multiple databases** are available. It's a good idea to find out if the system can connect to different databases and troubleshoot virtual machines and remote hosts. This is a tool that the programmer may find highly beneficial and time-saving.

- **Automation**. Specific tools within debugging systems could be automated, such as code completion. This would be a very convenient tool for the programmer and is worth inquiring about.

Debugger Features

The debugger allows users to debug programs written in languages that are finally generated into Base Language/Java.

MPS java debugger offers the following features:

1. **Execution**

   - executing local run configurations under debugger
   - connecting to a remote application

2. **Breakpoints**

   - line breakpoints
   - breakpoints viewer

3. **Runtime**

   - current debugger position highlighted in the editor
   - viewing and exporting threads state
   - viewing variables on stack frame
   - step-by-step execution (stepping over/into/out)
   - low-level expressions evaluation

Advantages and Disadvantages

- **Advantages**

  o It is single-step through the code.

  o It stops execution at a given point to investigate where it goes and what the values are.

  o It attaches to an already running program.

- **Disadvantages**

  o It is not running in real time, so it may not expose all problems.

LINTING

More and more developer teams have adopted linters and other static tools in their development tool, and some of them are integrated. So here we will see what a linter is, what it does, and why it is essential for you and your development team. It highlights syntactical and stylistic problems in your Python code, which often helps you identify and correct programming errors or unconventional coding practices that can occur to mistakes. For example, it detects the use of missing parentheses, uninitialized, or undefined variable, calls to fuzzy functions, and even more subtle issues such as attempting to redefine built-in types or functions. It is distinct from formatting because linting analyzes how the code runs and detects errors, whereas formatting analyzes how code appears. By default, its stylistic and syntactical code detection is enabled. If you require third-party linters for other problems detection, you can help them by using the Python: Select Linter command and selecting the appropriate linter. You can enable and disable all Linting by using the Python: Enable Linting command.

What Is a Linter?

It is a tool to help you improve your code, automated checking of source code from programmatic, stylistic errors.

Why Is Linting Important?

Linting is necessary to reduce errors and improve the quality of your code. Using these tools can help you can speed up the development and reduce the costs by finding mistakes.

How Does a Lint Tool Work?

- Write the code.
- Compile it.
- Analyze the code with the linter.
- Review the bugs identified by the tool.
- Make changes to the code to resolve the bugs.
- Link the modules once the code is clean.
- Analyze the code again with the linter.
- Take a review of the code.

When to Use the Lint Software

This only depends on your programming language. If you are using the interpreted programming languages, then you must be using lint software. Taking Python and JavaScript, both are the interpreted language, and they lack a compiling phase. So in that case using lint software will be effective for ensuring coding style and resolving basic coding errors.

Basic Lint Tools

These tools are the most common form of static analysis. Using lint tools can be beneficial for identifying common errors, such as:

- Indexing beyond arrays
- Dereferencing null pointers
- (Potentially) dangerous data type combinations
- Unreachable code
- Non-portable constructs

Enable Linters in the VS Code

For enabling linter in VS code, open the Command Palette (Ctrl + Shift + P) and select the Python: Select Linter command. This will add "Python. linting.<linter>Enabled": proper to your settings, as<linter> is the name of the chosen linter; for enabling a linter prompt you have to install the required packages in your selected workspace. For disabling, go to the Python: Enable Linting command, which shows a dropdown with the current linting state and options to turn Python linting off.

To perform linting you need to understand that the

- Linting can run automatically when you save a file.

- Whenever you open the Command Palette (Ctrl + Shift + P), enter and select Python: Run Linting.

General Linting Settings

This part describes settings for linting in specific linters; you can add any of the locations to your user settings.json file (by opening the file > Preferences > Settings command Ctrl + ,).

You can change the Python.linting.enabled for make in use. hen enabling lintOnSave, you might also want to allow the generic files.auto-Save option. This combination provides you frequent Linting feedback in your code while typing.

Specific Linters

Linter name	The package name for the pip install command
Pylint	pylint
Flake8	flake8
mypy	mypy
pycodestyle	pycodestyle
pylama	pylama
bandit	bandit

Lint attributes for a few languages like CSS, SCSS, Less in the workspace.

```
"css.lint.argumentsInColorFunction": "error"
"css.lint.boxModel": "ignore"
"css.lint.compatibleVendorPrefixes": "ignore"
"css.lint.float": "ignore"
"less.lint.boxModel": "ignore"
"less.lint.fontFaceProperties": "warning"
"scss.lint.float": "ignore"
"scss.lint.fontFaceProperties": "warning"
"scss.lint.idSelector": "ignore"
```

CHAPTER SUMMARY

In this chapter, we have covered one of the most important topics – debugging. Firstly, we got a basic introduction to debugging, then we discussed various methods of debugging with their tools. Topics like linting and JS Lint were also covered.

CHAPTER 7

VS Code Extensions

IN THIS CHAPTER

➢ Introduction to extension

➢ Commonly used extensions

In the previous chapter, we covered some topics related to debugging code and tools, linting, and JS unit linting, all of which help to accelerate your edit, compile, and debugging loop. But in this chapter, we will be covering many popular extensions in the Visual Studio Marketplace.

Visual Studio Code provides us with many cool features that can enhance our code and could be very helpful while writing the program. One of the ways to achieve this is by using extensions that could be installed directly in the editor. This chapter lists some valuable and unique Visual Studio Code extensions that are helpful in web development.

WHAT IS VS CODE MARKETPLACE?

Visual Studio has a new site for extensions called Visual Studio Marketplace, and this site will aggregate extensions for the Visual Studio, Visual Studio Code, and Visual Studio Team Services.

There are more than 7,000 extensions available in the Marketplace for Visual Studio. Most of these extensions were imported from Visual Studio Gallery.

DOI: 10.1201/9781003311973-7

How to Open VS Code Marketplace?

Clicking on the Extensions in the activity bar on the left side of VS Code or View: Extensions command (using keyboard shortcut Ctrl + Shift + X) will show you a list of the several popular VS Code extensions in the VS Code Marketplace.

Extension Marketplace in Visual Studio Code

Extensions enhance the power of the Visual Studio Code editor and help you grow as a web developer and software engineer. These are the ones that you need to extend your Visual Studio Code functionality. The properties that Visual Studio Code includes out of the box are just the beginning. VS Code extensions allow you to add languages, debuggers, and tools to your installation to support your development workflow. Its rich extensibility model lets extension authors plug directly into the VS Code User Interface and contribute functionality through the same APIs the VS Code uses. This chapter explains the new instance of VS Code and looks at the best extensions, why you should be using them, how to find, install, and manage everything about the VS Code extensions from the Visual Studio Code Marketplace.

Let's Start with How to Browse for the Extensions

The first thing we are going to do is open VS Code. You will find the extensions view on your activity bar just by hovering over the icon. You can also use the keyboard shortcut (Ctrl + Shift + X). The Extension automatically opens up on the sidebar.

You can browse and install many of the extensions from within VS Code. Just by bringing the extension view by clicking the Extension's icon on the activity bar. Figure 7.1 shows the Extension view icon (Figure 7.1).

Clicking on the icon will display a list of the most popular VS Code extensions in the VS Code Marketplace (Figure 7.2).

FIGURE 7.1 Extension icon in Visual Studio Code.

FIGURE 7.2   Recommended extensions in VS Code.

In Figure 7.2, you will see that if you click extension view, you will be shown some of the extensions already installed in your Visual Studio Code in the first section and some recommendations for you in the second section. Over the search bar, you can get your desired theme or Extension. Each Extension in the list will include a brief description, the publisher of that theme, the total download count, and a five-star rating. You can also select the extension item to display the extension details pages to learn more about the theme.

How to Install an Extension?

To install any extension in VS Code, click the Install button. After the installation is complete, the Install button will change to the manage gear button (Figure 7.3).

Find and Install an Extension

Let's have a look at the various Extension of the VS Code Marketplace in depth.

BRACKET PAIR COLORIZER EXTENSION

This extension allows you to match the brackets to identify with various color coding. The user can easily define which character to check and which color to use in the file (Figure 7.4).

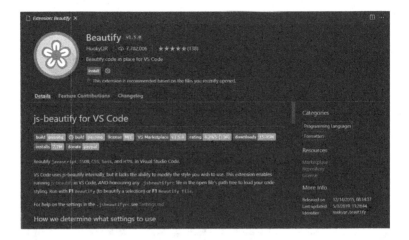

FIGURE 7.3   Installation of extensions from Marketplace.

FIGURE 7.4   Bracket Pair colonizer extension in Marketplace.

Figure 7.4 is of the Bracket Pair colorizer extension. This extension adds the highlighted lines linking brackets character like [] .i.e. square bracket), {} .i.e. Curly bracket, .i.e. () .i.e. parentheses, so that you can see your code section easily. For example, this code is the example of the templating engine, but you do not need to focus on the code. Just see the color of the brackets and text which has been written. To see that the Bracket Pair Colorize extension is working, open any source code files with nested regions. You will see the highlighting lines and different colors for matching bracket characters. As you make a move with your cursor around the editor, the highlighted enclosing region will change.

```
{{#if error_message}}
<br>
<div class="alert alert-danger">
{{error_message}}
</div>
{{/if}}
```

You can quickly identify the brackets of the particular sections like the if or <div> tag section. Another example of function brackets is

FIGURE 7.5 Bracket extension expands or reduces the text.

FIGURE 7.6 User setting option in the Workspace.

given below. Besides visual editor highlighting, the Bracket Pair extension also contributes several commands, Expand Bracket Selection and Undo Bracket Selection, that you can find in the Commands Palette (Ctrl + Shift + P) (Figure 7.5).

```
app.use(function(req, res, next){
res.locals.currentUser = req.user;
res.locals.error = req.flash("error");
res.locals.success = req.flash("success");
next();
});
```

This Extension also provides the setting for tuning its behavior, which you can find in the settings editor (Ctrl +,) (Figure 7.6).

If an extension doesn't give you the functionality you want, you can always uninstall the Extension from the manage button in the context menu. This is only just a straightforward example of how to install and use an extension. The VS Code Marketplace has hundreds and thousands of extensions supporting hundreds of programming languages and tasks.

Everything from fully featured and supported for Java, Go, C++, and Python to simple extensions that create rs, change the color theme, or add virtual pets.

Extension Details

Extension details provides you with full details of that particular Extension and a review of the wings.

- **Details:** In the detail section, you can get information about the new extension version on GitHub.

- **Feature contributions:** The extension's additions to Visual Studio Code include settings, commands, keyboard shortcuts, language grammar, debugger, etc.

- **Change log:** The extension repository CHANGELOG, if available also with the release notes of the version.

- **Dependencies:** It lists if the extension depends on any other extensions.

- **Runtime Status:** It tells you the activation time of the extension.

If an extension is an Extension Packteh, the Extension Pack section will display which extension will be installed when you have installed the package. All the Extension Pack bundles package their extensions together so they can be easily installed at one time.

Extension View Filter and Commands

You can filter the Extension view in the Filter Extension context menu.
Here is the list of filters you will get:

- The list of extensions currently installed

- The list of outdated extensions can be updated

- The list of presently enabled/disabled extensions

- The list of recommended advanced extensions based on your workspace

- The list of most popular extensions

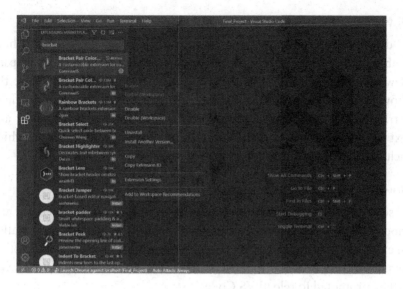

FIGURE 7.7   Extension view filter and commands.

You can also sort the extension list by Count or Rating in ascending or descending order. You can learn more about the extension search filter below.

You can run the addition Extension view command via the View and More Actions button. Through this context menu, you can take at your extension updates and enable behavior (Figure 7.7).

How to Search for an Extension?

You can empty the search box at the top of the Extensions view and type in the name of the extension, tool, or programming language you're looking for.

How to Manage Extensions

Visual Studio Code makes it easy to manage your extensions. You can install the Extension, disable all the installed extensions, updates, and uninstall extensions through the Extensions view, Start Extension Bisect, the Command Palette (commands have the Extensions: prefix), or command-line switches.

For example, typing "React" will bring up a list of all React language extensions.

How Do You List All the Installed Extensions?

By default, the Extensions view shows the extensions you presently have enabled, all extensions that are recommended for you, and a collapsed view of all extensions you have disabled previously. You can also use the Show Installed Extensions command, available in the Command Palette (Ctrl + Shift + P) or the More Actions (...) dropdown menu, to clear any text in the search box and show the list of all installed extensions, which includes those that have been disabled.

How to Uninstall an Extension?

By selecting the Manage gear button at the right of an extension entry and choosing Uninstall from the dropdown menu to uninstall, you installed an extension. You will be given two options: uninstall and Install another version of this particular Extension. After uninstalling the Extension you will be prompted to reload VS Code.

How to Disable an Extension

If you do not want to remove an extension permanently, you can disable the Extension temporarily by clicking the gear button at the right of an extension. You can disable an extension entirely or just for your currently active workspace. You will get a prompt to reload VS Code once after you disable an extension.

If you want to disable all installed extensions quickly, there is a Disable All Installed Extensions command in the Command Palette and, for more actions, dropdown menu.

Extensions remain disabled for all Visual Studio Code sessions until you re-enable them.

How to Enable an Extension

Similarly, if you have disabled an extension (in the Disabled section of the list and marked Disabled), you can re-enable it with the Enable or Enable (Workspace) commands in the dropdown menu.

How to Enable Extension Auto-Update

VS Code checks for the extension updates and installs them automatically. After updating, you will be prompted to reload VS Code. If you'd instead update your extensions manually, you can disable auto-update with the Disable Auto-Updating Extensions command that sets the extensions.

Auto-update setting to false. If you do not want VS Code to even check for updates, you can select the extensions. Auto-check updates setting to false.

How to Update an Extension Manually

If you have an Extension of auto-update disabled, you can quickly look for extension updates using the show outdated extensions command using this @outdated filter. This will display available updates for your installed extensions. Select the Update button for the outdated Extension and the update will be installed, and you will be prompted to reload VS Code. You can also update all your obsolete extensions one at a time with the Update All Extensions command. If you have automatic checking for updates disabled, you can use the Check for Extension Updates command to check which extensions can be updated.

How to Configure Extensions

VS Code extensions may have various configurations and requirements. Some of the extensions contribute settings to VS Code, which can be modified in the settings editor. Other extensions may have their configuration files. Extensions may also require installing and setting up extra components such as compilers, command-line tools, and debuggers. Check the Extension l visible in the Extensions view details page, or you can go to the extension page on the VS Code Marketplace. Many extensions are free to open source and have a link to their repository on the Marketplace page.

Recommended Extensions

You can able to see a list of recommended extensions using Show Recommended Extensions, which sets the @recommended filter. Extension recommendations can be:

- **Workspace Recommendations:** It is recommended by other users of your current workspace.

- **Other Recommendations:** It is recommended based on recently opened files.

See the section below to know how to contribute recommendations for other users in your project.

Command-Line Extension Management of the Extensions

To make it easier to configure VS Code, it is possible to list, install, and uninstall extensions using the command prompt. When identifying an extension, give the full name of the publisher. Extension, for example, ms-python. Python.

Command Line	Description
code --extensions-dir <dir>	It sets the root path for extensions.
code --list-extensions	It lists all the installed extensions.
code --show-versions	It shows versions of installed extensions when using --list-extension.
code --install-extension (<extension-id> | <extension-vsix-path>)	Installs an extension.
code --uninstall-extension (<extension-id> | <extension-vsix-path>)	Uninstalls an extension.
code --enable-proposed-api (<extension-id>)	It enables API features for extensions. It can receive one or more extension IDs to help individually.

What Are Extensions View Filters?

The Extension's search box supports filters that help to find and manage extensions. You have seen filters such as @recommended and @installed, and if you used the commands Show Recommended Extensions and Show Installed Extensions. There are various filters available for sorting by ratings and search by category (example, "Linters"), tags (for example, "node"). You will see a full list of filters and sort commands by typing @ in the extensions search box and navigating through the suggestions (Figure 7.8):

Here are the Extensions view filters:

- **@builtin:** It shows extensions that come with VS Code. Grouped by type (Programming Languages, Themes, etc.).

- **@disabled:** It shows disabled installed extensions.

- **@installed:** It shows installed extensions.

- **@outdated:** It shows outdated installed extensions. The latest version is available on the Marketplace.

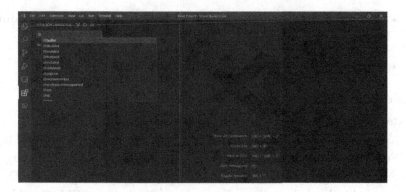

FIGURE 7.8   View filters of extension.

- **@enabled:** It shows enabled installed extensions. Extensions can be individually enabled/disabled.

- **@recommended:** It shows recommended extensions. Grouped as workspace specific or general use.

- **@category:** It shows extensions belonging to a specified category. Below are a few of the supported categories. For a whole list, type @ category and follow the options in the list:

  o **@category:** formatters

  o **@category:** linters

  o **@category:** themes

  o **@category:** snippets

These filters can be combined as well. Example: Use the @installed and @ category: themes to view all installed themes.

When no filter is provided, the Extensions view displays the currently installed and recommended extensions.

Sorting Extension

You can also sort your extensions with the @sort filter, which can take the following values:

- **Installs:** Sorting by Marketplace installation count, in descending order.

- **Rating:** Sorting by Marketplace rating (1–5 stars), in descending order.

- **Name:** Sorting alphabetically by extension name.

Categories and Tags in Extension

Extensions can be set as categories and tags describing their features.

You can also apply filters on category and tag by using variety: and tag.

Supported categories are Snippets, Linters, Programming Languages, Themes, Debuggers, and Other, Extension Packs, Language Packs, Data Science, Machine Learning, Formatters, Keymaps, SCM Providers, Visualization, and Notebooks. They can be accessed by the IntelliSense in the extensions search box (Figure 7.9).

Install from a VSIX

In Visual Studio Code, you can manually install packaged in a .vsix file. The Install from VSIX command in the Extension view command dropdown, or the Extension: Install from VSIX command in the Command Palette, point to the .vsix file.

You can also install it using the VS Code --install-extension command-line switch providing the path to the .vsix file.

```
code --install-extension myextension.vsix
```

You can install --install-extension multiple times on the command line to install multiple extensions at once.

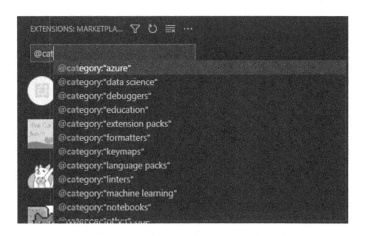

FIGURE 7.9   Categories and tags.

If you would like to learn more about packaging and publishing extensions, see our Publishing Extensions article in the Extension API.

Workspace Recommended Extensions

A set of extensions can make working with a particular workspace or programming language more productive, and you would often like to share this list with your team or colleagues. You can create a list of extensions for a workspace with the Extensions: Configure Recommended Extensions (Workspace Folder) command.

In a single directory workspace, that command creates an extensions.js on file located in the Workspace. vscode folder where you can add a list of extensions ({publisherName}. {extensionName}).

In a multi-root workspace, the command opens your .code-workspace file, where you can list extensions. Recommendations. You can add extension recommendations to individual folders in a multi-root workspace by using the Extensions: Configure Recommended Extensions (Workspace Folder) command.

An example extensions.json is:

```
{
    "recommendations": ["dbaeumer.vscode-eslint",
    "esbenp.prettier-vscode"]
}
```

Which recommends a linter extension and with a code formatter extension.

An extension is identified with its publisher name and Extension identifier publisher. Extension. You can see the name on the particular extension detail page. VS Code will provide you with auto-completion for installed extensions inside these files.

If any virus-scanned in any extension.

The extension is removed from the Marketplace.

The extension is added to the kill list so that if installed, it will be automatically uninstalled by VS Code.

How to Stop VS Code from Providing Extension Recommendations in VS Code?

Yes, if you would prefer not to have VS Code display extension recommendations in the Extensions view or through notifications, you can change the following settings:

- **extensions.showRecommendationsOnlyOnDemand:** Set to true to remove the Recommended section.

- **extensions.ignore recommendations:** It is set to true to silence extension recommendation notifications.

The Show Recommended Extensions command is always available if you want to see recommendations.

Are Extensions from the Marketplace Secure?

It runs a virus scan on each extension package that is published. Each time an Extension is installed or updated a virus scan is conducted.

ONE DARK PRO EXTENSION FOR VISUAL STUDIO CODE

Now, let's install the popular One Dark Pro (Atom) extension. Let's search for that Extension in the search bar (Figure 7.10).

You will see the many extensions already showing there; look at some options. We first need to head over to the search up here and grab ourselves a perfect one for your Visual Studio Code. The popular theme in the Marketplace is Atom Theme with its dark mode. When you search the Atom search, you will get various options like Atom Dark Theme, JavaScript Atom Grammar, Atom One Dark Syntax Theme, Atom Keymap, etc. But here we are, just looking at One Dark pro (Figure 7.11).

With this version, you get a lot of cool stuff. If you look down here, you get a lot of good coloring for classes, functions, methods, and variables in JavaScript. This is very distinct. This makes coding much more straight-forward, and install this, and we click install. Immediately it's available to us. This is already looking way better. Here we have just that extension in VS Code. The dark theme has a lot of benefits like it having very harsh light on your eyes the dark mode makes coding easier you can able to spend time more on the screen that why we prefer this that you should install it and work as long you want to and also good for your eyes especially in the night time, it helps a lot (Figure 7.12).

AUTO-CLOSE TAG EXTENSION FOR VISUAL STUDIO CODE

This is a great extension. It is straightforward so let's quickly install it and have a look at it. It will close any of the tags that you have created if you

FIGURE 7.10 Searching Atom extension in the search bar.

FIGURE 7.11 One Dark Pro extension.

are writing any code. For example, if your code is in the HTML language, it will return you the closing tag for HTML, same with the other tags it is most beneficial. In short, the auto-close tag extension automatically adds HTML/XML close tag, same as in Visual Studio Sublime text (Figure 7.13).

The VS Code 1.16 version has built-in close tag support for Handlebars, HTML, and Razor files. This extension is enabled for other languages like

FIGURE 7.12   Description of One Dark Pro extension inside the window.

Vue, JavaScript, XML, PHP, TypeScript, JSX, TSX, etc. It can be configurable (Figure 7.14).

Some Features of Auto-Close Extension

- It automatically adds a closing tag when you type in the closing bracket of the opening tag.

- It automatically closes the self-closing tag.

- After any closing tag is inserted, the cursor is between the opening and closing tag.

- It supports auto close tag as Sublime Text 3.

- It uses Keyboard Shortcut or Command Palette to add the close tag manually.

- It set the tag list that would not be auto closed.

Usage

After typing in the closing of the opening tag, the closed one will be added automatically. To add a close tag manually, you can type and use the keyboard shortcut as Alt + . (in Windows). In Mac, we use (Command + Alt + .)

FIGURE 7.13   Auto-close extension.

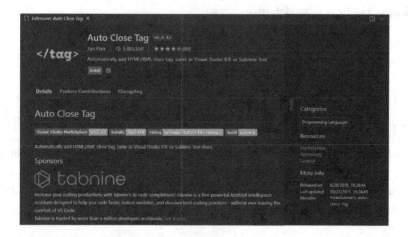

FIGURE 7.14   Auto-close extension details.

SUBLIME TEXT 3 MODE EXTENSION FOR VISUAL STUDIO CODE

To add the closing tag automatically, set the below configuration from false to true:

```
{
  "auto-close-tag.SublimeText3Mode": true
}
```

This setting is false to default.

Configuration

Use "auto-close-tag.enableAutoCloseTag" to set whether to insert close tag automatically.

```
{
  "auto-close-tag.enableAutoCloseTag ":true
}
```

To set self-closing tag automatically will be added automatically if below setting is true:

```
{
  "auto-close-tag.enableAutoCloseSelfClosingTag":
true
}
```

If you would like to insert a space before the forward slash in a self-closing tag (it is false default):

```
{
"auto-close-tag".insertSpaceBeforeSelfCosingTag":
false
}
```

SETTINGS SYNC EXTENSION FOR VISUAL STUDIO CODE

It lets you share your Visual Studio Code Configuration such as crucial key binding, installed Extensions, and changes settings so that you can always work with your favorite setup. This feature was added to VS Code in July 2020 (Figure 7.15).

FIGURE 7.15   Settings Sync extension in VS Code.

1. Search for Settings Sync in the Command Palette.

   In mac, ⌘ + Shift + P

   In Linux and Window, Ctrl + Shift + P

2. Turn on Settings Sync and sign in.

   You can sign in using Microsoft/Git account. You can choose what to sync & what to not.

3. After logging in, settings sync should be turned on, and you are now syncing to your account. Repeat the same process on each of your devices.

Issues When Syncing

When you sync your Visual Studio Code settings, it might happen. The available options are:

- **Merge:** It attempts to merge local settings with the remote settings.
- **Replace local:** It overwrites the local environment with the small settings.
- **Merge manually:** It merges preferences manually one by one.

Features of Settings Sync

- It uses your GitHub account token and Gist.
- It is easy to upload and download with a single click.

- Show a summary page at the end with details about config and extensions affected.

- The auto-download Latest Settings on Startup and auto upload settings on file change.

- It shares the Gist with other users and lets them download your settings.

- It supports GitHub Enterprise.

- It supports pragmas with @sync keywords: host, os, and env are supported.

- It helps you to change GUI for changing settings/logging in.

- It allows you to sync any file across your machines.

Keyboard Shortcut

- **Upload Key:** Shift + Alt + U

- **Download Key:** Shift + Alt +D

- **Upload your settings:** Shift + Alt + U

- **Download your setting:** Shift + Alt + D

REACT NATIVE TOOLS EXTENSION FOR VISUAL STUDIO CODE

It is an extension of Visual Studio Code. It offers you a helpful environment for developing React Native projects. It supports and helps the developers during the code debugging process. This free tool runs the react-native command using the Command Palette. Microsoft developed it.

About the Extension

In VS Code extension that provides you a development environment for React Native projects. Using this Extension, you can quickly debug your code and run react-native commands from the Command Palette.

Now, let's install this Extension React Native Tool extension. Let's search that Extension in the search bar (Figure 7.16).

You will see the many extensions already showing there; look at some options. We first need to head over to the search box in your Visual Studio Code editor. A popular theme in the Marketplace is React Native

FIGURE 7.16   React Native Tool extension in the search bar.

Extension. When you search the React Native tool, you will get various options like React Native Snippet, Simple React Snippets, etc. But here we are just looking at React Native Tools (Figure 7.17).

FIGURE 7.17   React Native Tool extension details.

GIT LENS EXTENSION FOR VISUAL STUDIO CODE

It changes the Git capabilities built into VS Code. It helps to visualize code authorship at a glance via Git blame annotations and code lens, navigate and explore Git repositories, gain valuable insights via powerful comparison commands, and so on.

This Extension if one of the most popular in the community and is also the most powerful. It can replace each of the previous two extensions with its functionality.

It is powerful, feature-rich, and highly customizable to meet your needs. It helps you better understand code. Here are some of the features of GitLens.

Effortless revision navigation through the history of the file, authorship code lens, a status bar blame, rich remote providers integrations, many powerful commands for navigating and comparing revision, and more, user-defined modes for quickly toggling between sets of settings.

Here are some of the features that GitLens provides:

- It has effortless revision navigation (backward and forward).

- The current line blame annotation at the end of the line shows the commit and author who last modified the line, with more detailed blame information accessible on the hover.

- Its authorship code lens shows the most recent commit and number of authors at the top of files and on code blocks.

- File annotations in the editor

  1. **blame:** It shows the commit and author who last modified each line of a file.

  2. **changes:** It highlights any local (unpublished) changes or lines changed by the most recent commit.

  3. **heatmap:** It shows how recently lines were changed, relative to all the other changes in the file.

GitLens Settings

Name	Description
gitlens.currentLine.dateFormat	It specifies how to format absolute dates.
gitlens.currentLine.enabled	It specifies whether to provide a blame annotation for the current line.
gitlens.currentLine.format	It specifies the format of the current line blame annotation.
gitlens.currentLine.scrollable	It specifies whether the current line blame annotation can be scrolled into view when it is outside the viewport.

Git Code Lens Settings

gitlens.codeLens.authors. command	gitlens.toggleFileChanges – It toggles file changes since before the commit.
	gitlens.toggleFileChangesOnly – It toggles file changes from the commit.
	gitlens.diffWithPrevious – It opens changes with the previous revision.
	gitlens.revealCommitInView – It reveals the commit in the Side Bar.
	gitlens.showCommitsInView – It searches for commits within the range.
	gitlens.showQuickCommitDetails – It shows details of the commit.
	gitlens.showQuickCommitFileDetails – It show file details of the commit.
	gitlens.showQuickFileHistory – It shows the current file history.
gitlens.codeLens.authors. enabled	It specifies whether to provide an author's code lens, showing the number of authors of the file.
gitlens.codeLens.enabled	It specifies whether to provide any Git code lens by default.

CSS PEEK EXTENSION FOR VISUAL STUDIO CODE

This extension widens HTML and EJS code editing with Go To Definition and Go To Symbol in workspace support for CSS/SCSS/LESS (classes and IDs) found in strings within the source code.

A similar feature heavily inspired this in the code editor brackets called CSS Inline Editors. It also Extension supports all the capabilities of symbol definition tracking but does it for CSS selectors (classes, IDs, and HTML tags). This will include:

1. **Peek:** It is used to load the CSS file inline and make quick edits (Ctrl + Shift + F12).

2. **Go To:** It is used to jump directly to the CSS file or open it in a new editor (F12).

3. **Hover:** It is used to show the definition in a hover over the text or symbol (Ctrl + hover) (Figure 7.18).

Some Configurations

1. **cssPeek.supportsTags:** It enables peeking from the HTML tags to class and unique IEDs.

FIGURE 7.18   CSS Peek extension in VS Code.

2. **CssPeekFromLangauge:** It is the list of all the VS Code languages where the Extension should be used.

3. **cssPeek.peekToExclude:** It is the list of filter-out style files to not look for.

Live Server

Installation

You can skip this if you already have VS Code on your computer unless you can download it from its official website.

After you've downloaded and installed VS Code, you are going to see the welcome screen.

On the left side, you should see a couple of icons. One of them is the extensions button.

Once you click on it, a search bar will appear. Just type in, "live server". (Figure 7.19).

PRETTIER EXTENSION FOR VISUAL STUDIO CODE

It is an opinionated code formatter, enforces a consistent style by parsing your code and reprinting its own rules that take the max line length into the code with necessary. It supports various languages.

- HTML

- JSON

- JSX

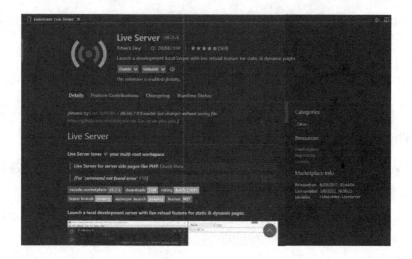

FIGURE 7.19   Live server extension.

- JavaScript

- Flow

- YAML

- Vue

- CSS, Less, and SCSS

- GraphQLES2017

It helps to remove all the original styling and ensure the outputted code conforms to a consistent style, and guarantees consistency by parsing JavaScript into an AST and pretty-printing the AST.

Note: Everything is fixable.

It takes your code and reprints it from scratch by taking the line length. for example,

Function foo(arg1, arg2, arg3, arg4, agr5)

It fits in a single line easily as below:

foo(Funtcion2(), Funtcion3(), Funtcion4(), Funtcion5());

Prettier Versions

Version	Install with	Documentation
2.4.1	npm install prettier	stable
2.5.0-dev	Npm install prettier/prettier	next

Why Do We Use Prettier?

- Building and enforcing a style guide is prettier because it is the only "style guide" that is fully automatic.

- It is usually introduced by people having more experience in the current codebase and JavaScript.

- Easy to adopt.

- Clean up an existing codebase.

Why Should I Use the Live-Server Extension?

Usually, when you change your code or write something, you need to refresh the page manually to see the effects. In other words, if you make 20 changes in your code each day, you need to refresh the browser 20 times. The live-server extension can do this automatically for you. After installing it, computerized localhost will run in your browser, which you can start with a single click. When you make changes in your code or write something new, the browser will auto-refresh itself after saving it. Then you will be able to see the changes quickly and automatically.

Installation of Prettier
First, install Prettier locally:

npm	yarn
npm install --save-dev --save-exact prettier	yarn add --dev --exact prettier

Then, to create an empty config file, let editors and other tools know you are using Prettier:

```
echo {}> .prettierrc.JSON
```

Next, create a .prettierignore to let the Prettier CLI and editors know which files to not format. Here is an example:

Ignore artifacts:

build

coverage

Base your if you have one of these .prettierignore on .gitignore and .eslintignore.

Now, do format all files with Prettier:

npm	yarn
npm prettier --write	yarn prettier --write

It (prettier –write) is excellent for formatting everything, but it might take a little long time for a big project.

Some essential points of Prettier:

- Install the same version of Prettier locally in your project to ensure that everyone gets the same version of Prettier; even a patch release of it can result in slightly different formatting.

- Add a .prettierrc.JSON file to let your code editor know that you are using it in your project.

- Add a .prettierignore file to let your code editor know which files are not to touch, as well as for being able to run prettier --write. To format the entire project.

- Run prettier --check-in CI (command line) to ensure that your project stays formatted.

- Run Prettier only from your code editor for the best experience.

- Use eslint-config-prettier to make it and ESLint play nicely together.

- Now, set up a pre-commit hook to make sure that every commit is formatted correctly.

Snippets

This Extension contains all the coding snippets for JavaScript in ES6 syntax for VS Code editor (supports both JavaScript and TypeScript even more). All the snippets include the final semicolon (;).

Installation

In order to install an extension you have to launch the using these keyboard shortcut (Ctrl + Shift + P or Cmd + Shift + P) Command Palette and (Ctrl + Shift + P or Cmd + Shift + P) then type "Extensions". There two options will be shown as already installed snippets or new ones. Search for JavaScript (ES6) code snippets and install them.

Supported Languages File Extensions

- JavaScript (.js)

- TypeScript (.ts)

- JavaScript React (.jsx)

- TypeScript React (.tsx)

- Html (.html)

- Vue (.vue)

Here below is a list of all currently available snippets and the triggers of each one. It →ι means the hit TAB key.

Class helper

Trigger	Content
pge→	adds default constructor in the class constructor() {}
met→	creates a method inside a class add() {}
con→	creates a getter property get propertyName() {return value;}
pse→	creates a setter property set propertyName(value) {}

Console Method

Trigger	Content
cas→	It console alert method console.assert(expression, object)
cco→	console count console.count(label)
cdb→	It console debug console.debug(object)
cdi→	It console dir console.dir
Acer→	It console error console.error(object)

(Continued)

Trigger	Content
cgr→	It console group console.group(label)
cge→	console groupEnd console.groupEnd()
clg→	It console log console.log(object)
clo→	It console log object with name console.log("object :>> ", object);
ctr→	It console trace console.trace(object)
C→	It console warn console. warn
cin→	It console info console.info
clt→	It Console table console.table
cti→	It console time console.time
cte→	It console timeEnd console.timeEnd

LIVE SASS COMPILER EXTENSION FOR VS CODE

Live Sass Compiler will compile your sass into CSS now we have a sass for beginners. Let's open up the extension and scroll down, or you can search for an extension in VS Code Marketplace called Live Sass Compiler Extension and install it. If you press Ctrl +, get to the settings, and just type in "sass", you should see the Live Sass Compiler in the index of the setting, then edit the Settings.json file.

To run your sass project, you have to create a file with the Extension .scss and save it. The status bar will have to get Live Sass on the bottom right corner. Just press that, and your live server runs.

There Are Some Shortcuts for SASS

- Click to Watch Sass from the Status bar to turn on the live compilation and then click Stop Watching Sass from the status bar.

- **Press F1 or Ctrl + Shift + P and type Live Sass:** Watch sass to start live server compilation or, type Live Sass: Stop Watching Sass stop a live server compilation.

- **Press F1 or Ctrl+ Shift + P and type Live Sass:** Compile Sass - Without Watch Mode to compile Sass or Sass for one time.

Feature of Live Sass Compiler

- It provides the Live SASS & SCSS Compile.

- The customizable file location of exported CSS.

- It has customizable exported CSS Styles like expanded, compact, compressed, nested.

- It has customizable extension name (.css or .min.css).

- Quick status bar control.

- It excludes Specific Folders by settings.

- The live Reload to browser dependency on Live Server extension.

- It supports the Auto prefix.

Installation

Open Visual Studio Code Editor and Press Ctrl+ P, type ext install live-sass.

REST Client

This extension is beneficial for a frontend developer or even for a Full Stack developer. When working with a back-end API, we can get that response from within VS Code if you want to see what that API response is. This extension is so similar to a program called postman. Postman is the external program. The main benefit of using this Extension is that it's all in VS Code editor. You do not need to install a separate program. The way this Extension works is it allows you to send HTTP requests and view the response in Visual Studio Code directly.

Usage

In the editor, create a new file new Request.HTTP then in that file write the GET and POST methods

GET https://jsonplaceholder.tyicode.com/posts, and this method returns the stored data as a result.

POST https://jsonplaceholder.typicode.com/posts Content-Type: application/JSON. This method will help you to store data.

```
{
"title": "New Post".
"body": "This is a new post."
}
```

Once you are done with this code, for the Send Request method, drag your mouse and hover over the POST and GET click. This method sends the Request, but will appear only if the file's language mode is HTTP; by default, .http files are like this. or you can use shortcut Ctrl + Alt + R In windows (Cmd + Alt +R for macOS) or by right-clicking in the editor and select Send Request in the menu, or by pressing F1 and then select/type Rest Client: Send Request. The response result will be shown in a separate webview panel right-hand side of Visual Studio Code. You can preview the response in an untitled document by setting rest-client. previewResponseInUntitledDocument to true in the setting file. Once a request is passed, the waiting spin icon will be displayed in the status bar until the response comes back. You can click the spin icon to terminate your request. Then, the icon will be replaced with the total duration and response size.

```
GET https://example.com/comments/1
###
GET https://example.com/topics/1
###
POST https://example.com/comments,
content-type: application/json
{
  "name": "demo",
  "time": "Wed, 21 Oct 2015 18:27:50 GMT"
}
```

You may want to save multiple requests in the same file and execute any of them efficiently. REST Client extension could help you recognize requests separated by lines beginning with three or more consecutive # as a delimiter. Place the cursor between the delimiters, issuing the Request as above, and the underlying Request will be sent out like the above example.

Workflow

Press F1t then type ext install, and now search for rest-client.

Request Line

GET https://example.com/comments

GET https://example.com/comments/1

https://example.com/comments/1

If the request method is made, the request will be treated as GET, so the above requests are the same after parsing.

Request Headers

The lines after the request line are parsed as Request Headers. Ensure that you provide headers with the standard field-name: field-value format. Each line represents one header. By default, this REST Client extension will add a User-Agent header with value vscode-restclient in your Request if you do not explicitly specify it. You can change the previously defined value in setting rest-client.defaultHeaders. Here are the examples of Request Headers:

```
User-Agent: rest-client
Accept-Language:
en-GB,en-US;q=0.8,en;q=0.6,zh-CN;q=0.4
Content-Type: application/json
```

QUOKKA.JS EXTENSION FOR VISUAL STUDIO CODE

It is an excellent extension that allows you to do speedy prototyping and testing in your js code, and it is not a single-purpose extension. It has tons of valuable features. It makes learning, exploring, and testing TypeScript and JavaScript fast. By default, no configuration is required; simply open a new Quokka file and start experimenting with what you want. You should focus on writing code instead of writing bespoke configuration files to try a simple idea or learn a new language feature. After installing the Quokka .js Extension, you can go ahead and use the command or Ctrl + Shift + P or F1 button and start typing "Quokka". Then, you will see many options there. To create a new JavaScript file, if you have a project, you can run Quokka on it directly using the Quakka.js: Start on Current File option. As you create a new file, you will notice down there in your terminal as,

```
Quokka 'Untitled-1.js' (node: v14.15.0, babel:
v7.15.8, plugins: auto-detect:create-react-app,
jsdom-quokka-plugin)
```

It is going to show your code and possible errors.

If you write anything or suddenly make a mistake, it warns you to side by side in the console.

Example:

```
Const
```

In the above example, you will see I write just a const keyword and down in the terminal, and you will see the below as a result:

```
Quokka 'Untitled-1.js' (node: v14.15.0, babel:
v7.15.8, plugins: auto-detect:create-react-app,
jsdom-quokka-plugin)
SyntaxError: .\quokka.js: Unexpected token (1:6)
> 1 | const
  |      ^
```

This is the output of the above code. It won't fix until you fix it. So, let's assign value to const and write variable.

```
const a= 1
```

So here I assign the variable as 1, then in the output, you will find nothing.

```
Quokka 'Untitled-1.js' (node: v14.15.0, babel:
v7.15.8, plugins: auto-detect:create-react-app,
jsdom-quokka-plugin)
```

Its 'Community' edition is free for everyone, brought to you by the Wallaby.js developing team. While working on the Wallaby.js product, you will face thousands of complex problems and JavaScript code execution. It (Quokka) uses the same technology as Wallaby.js.

CODESNAP EXTENSION FOR VISUAL STUDIO CODE

It allows you to take a screenshot of your code blocks. Run Ctrl + Shift + p (Command Palette) search codesnap in it. If your VS Code has this extension, you will search options; otherwise, install it from the extension marketplace.

Once done with your installation, open that in the Command Palette and type codesnap the window panel it displays on the right side. When you select your code, your code chosen will say on that window with color texting, alignment. Adjust the screenshot width, and then click the shutter button to save the screenshot in your system.

Feature

- If you can get screenshots of your code quickly, and can be easily saved.

- It can also copy the screenshots to your clipboard.

- Also, show numbers of line.

- Also, have many other configuration options.

COLOR HIGHLIGHT FOR VISUAL STUDIO CODE

It is a handy extension if you use a lot of CSS in your file then. Using the help of this Extension, you can get the code color as simple. If the Extension highlights the color background, you need not hover over that color to get its color information. You can also change the settings of the color highlight of desire.

BETTER COMMENTS FOR VISUAL STUDIO CODE

This Better Comments extension will help you create more human-friendly comments in your program file. With this Extension, you will be able to categorize your annotations into various forms like:

- Alerts

- Highlights

- Queries

- TODOs

Commented out your code can also be styled to make it clear the code should not be helpful. It is just for getting the information about your code. Any other comment styles you would like to do, you can specify in the settings.

The following are examples of various annotations:

- – it is for highlighting

- ? – it is for questions

- ! – it is for warnings

- TODO – it is for todos

- //// – it is for line-through comments

Especially for the highlighting of warnings and todos, you will find this super helpful. It is pretty hard to miss when you read through the code.

Configuration Files

The extension can be configured in User Settings or Workspace Settings.

Configuration	Description
"better-comments.multilineComments": true	This setting will control whether multiline comments are styled using the annotation tags. When false, multiline statements will be presented without decoration.
"better-comments.highlightPlainText": false	This setting will control whether comments in a plain text file are styled using the annotation tags. When true, the tags (defaults: ! * ? //) will be detected if they're the first character on a line.
better-comments.tags	The tags are the characters or sequences used to mark a comment for decoration. The default five can be modified to change the colors, and more can be added.

The tags or symbol color can be changed by changing or adding the various settings.

```
"better-comments.tags": [
  {
  "tag": "!",
  "color": "#FF2D00",
  "strikethrough": false,
  "underline": false,
  "backgroundColor": "transparent",
  "bold": false,
  "italic": false
  },
  {
  "tag": "<>",
  "color": "#3498DB",
  "strikethrough": false,
  "underline": false,
  "backgroundColor": "transparent",
  "bold": false,
  "italic": false
  },
  {
  "tag": "+",
  "color": "#474747",
  "strikethrough": true,
  "underline": false,
  "backgroundColor": "transparent",
```

```
"bold": false,
"italic": false
},
{
"tag": "#",
"color": "#FF8C00",
"strikethrough": false,
"underline": false,
"backgroundColor": "transparent",
"bold": false,
"italic": false
},
{
"tag": "*",
"color": "#98C379",
"strikethrough": false,
"underline": false,
"backgroundColor": "transparent",
"bold": false,
"italic": false
}
]
```

Supported Languages

C, C#, C++, CoffeeScript, CSS, Dart, Dockerfile, GenStat, Go, GraphQL, Groovy, Haskell, Haxe, HiveQL, HTML, Java, JavaScript, JavaScript React, JSON with comments, Julia, Kotlin, LaTex (inlc. Bibtex/Biblatex), Less, Lisp, Lua, Makefile, Markdown, Nim, MATLAB, Objective-C, Objective-C++, PascalPerl, Perl 6, PHP, PowerShell, Puppet, Python, R, and so on.

Racket, Ruby, Rust, SAS, Sass, Scala, SCSS, ShellScript, SQL, STATA, Swift, Tcl, TypeScript, TypeScript React, Visual Basic, Vue.js, XML.

AUTO RENAME TAG FOR VISUAL STUDIO CODE

We are aware that most of the tags in HTML need a closing tag at the end (called paired tags) and writing professional code, which includes thousands of lines of code. Tags are closed after many of the lines. It becomes challenging to rename the tag. We have to find where the tag was closed. It provides us a feature that when we can change the starting tag, it will automatically adjust the closing tag.

Configuration

Add an extra entry into auto-rename-tag.activationOnLanguage to set the multiple languages at once the attributes used in the array that the Extension will be activated. By default, it is ["*"] and will be started for all languages.

```
{
  "auto-rename-tag.activationOnLanguage": ["html",
"xml", "php", "javascript"]
}
```

HTML BOILERPLATE FOR VISUAL STUDIO CODE

It is used to build faster and create standards-friendly sites every time. It is a set of files that provide a basic structure to any website built by industry professionals who have experienced similar issues and do not want others to have the same problems. HTML5 Boilerplate is the best place to start as a beginner. It describes as "the web's most popular frontend template" and a simple HTML template that boasts all the essential files and things you need to start building right away.

Usage

To install HTML5 Boilerplate, then open the Extension Marketplace (keyboard shortcut: Ctrl + Shift + X), search HTML5 Boilerplate. When you get this, install it. To check that it is working properly, create a new HTML file. When you start writing <html>, then you will see suggestions list of HTML, html5-boilerplate. Select html5-boilerplate, then hit Enter. You get the below code instantly as same.

```
<!DOCTYPE html>
<!--[if lt IE 7]>   <html class="no-js lt-ie9 lt-ie8
lt-ie7"> <![endif]-->
<!--[if IE 7]>   <html class="no-js lt-ie9 lt-ie8">
<![endif]-->
<!--[if IE 8]>   <html class="no-js lt-ie9">
<![endif]-->
<!--[if gt IE 8]>   <html class="no-js">
<!--<![endif]-->
<html>
  <head>
  <meta charset="utf-8">
```

```
<meta http-equiv="X-UA-Compatible"
content="IE=edge">
<title></title>
<meta name="description" content="">
<meta name="viewport" initial-scale=1"
content="width=device-width,>
<link rel="stylesheet" href="">
</head>
<body>
<!--[if lt IE 7]>
 <p class="browsehappy">You are using an
<strong>outdated</strong> browser. Please <a
href="#">upgrade your browser</a> to improve your
experience.</p>
<![endif]-->
<script src="" async defer></script>
</body>
</html>
```

INTENT RAINBOW FOR VISUAL STUDIO CODE

A simple little extension provides a colorized indentation in your coding with different colors for each level. In other languages like HTML, it makes indentation slightly more readable and thus becomes a little extra pleaser to read the code. Indentation is coming in the language syntax.

It is straightforward to change the colors of the indents.

Navigate to Settings, search for "colors" in the search bar, choose Appearance and click the 'Edit in settings.json" link. To find or create the property "indentRainbow.colors", add the colors to the array.

The examples of colors look like this:

```
// Defining custom color instead of default
"Rainbow" for dark backgrounds.
// (Changing them and restart the editor !)
"indentRainbow.colors": [
"rgba(16,16,16,0.1)",
"rgba(16,16,16,0.2)",
"rgba(16,16,16,0.3)",
"rgba(16,16,16,0.4)",
"rgba(16,16,16,0.5)",
"rgba(16,16,16,0.6)",
```

```
  "rgba(16,16,16,0.7)",
  "rgba(16,16,16,0.8)",
  "rgba(16,16,16,0.9)",
  "rgba(16,16,16,1.0)"
  ],
  // The indent color if the number of spaces is not
a multiple of "tabSize."
  "indentRainbow.errorColor": "rgba(128, 12, 12,0.6)"
  // The indent color when there's a mix between
spaces and tabs.
  // To be disabled, this coloring set this to an
empty string.
  "indentRainbow.tabmixColor": "rgba(128,32,96,0.6)"
}
// The indent color if the number of spaces is not a
multiple of "tabSize."
  "indentRainbow.errorColor": "rgba(128,32,32,0.6)"
  // The indent color when there is a mix between
spaces and tabs.
  // To be disabled, this coloring set this to an
empty string.
  "indentRainbow.tabmixColor": "rgba(128,32,96,0.6)"
```

Try out this extension. The link is given below:

https://marketplace.visualstudio.com/items?itemName=oderwat
.indent-rainbow

Configuration

```
// Languages indent-rainbow must be activated (if it
is empty, it means all languages will be included).
"indentRainbow.includedLanguages": [] // example
["nim", "nims", "python"]
// Languages indent-rainbow must be deactivated (if
it is empty, it means none or nothing).
"indentRainbow.excludedLanguages": ["text"]
// Delay should be in ms until the editor update.
"indentRainbow.updateDelay": 200 // Less value makes
it super fast but may cost more resources
```

Skip error highlighting for some languages. For example, you have to turn off the indent errors for markdown and Haskell (which is the default)

```
"indentRainbow.ignoreErrorLanguages" : [
"markdown",
"haskell"
]
```

DEBUGGER FOR CHROME FOR VISUAL STUDIO CODE

Debugging makes your web applications with Visual Studio Code more efficient. It helps you save time and keeps your code much nicer because you don't have to write a bunch of consoles.logs in JavaScript or another language.

The thing you need to do first is install the debugger for the Chrome extension in VS Code. After installation, you are almost ready to go. The next thing you need to do is create a launch file for the Visual Studio Code Debugger. This file mainly contains the debugger's various configurations for your project.

You can launch the file by going to the debug section in the activity bar.

If you have more debugger instead of Chrome, a list of options will prompt you to select the "Chrome" one. After installation or choosing your debugger environment, you will have a .vscode directory with a launch.json file.

There are two types of Chrome debugging configurations: launch and attach.

Launch

This configuration launches a Chrome instance running a particular file or URL. If you specify a URL, you need to set webRoot to the directory that files are served from. This can be an absolute path or a path using the ${workspaceFolder} resolver.

Things to understand:

- webRoot is used to resolve URLs
- ${workspaceFolder}, this can be an absolute path or a path

There are two launch configurations:

1. Launching against a local server

2. Launching against a local file

Attach

This will attach the debugger to a running instance of Chrome. You have to launch Chrome with remote debugging enabled for using it.

Supported Features

1. They are set up including breakpoints and source files when maps are enabled.

2. Stepping, including buttons on the Chrome page.

3. The Locals scope variables via the Locals pane.

4. Debugging eval scripts, script tags, and scripts that are added dynamically.

5. Watches via the Visual Studio Code watch panel.

6. The Debug Console.

7. TypeScript, via source maps.

Locals Turbo Console Log

It will automate the procedure of writing meaningful log messages. It is straightforward to highlight the variable you wish to log out, and then press Ctrl + Alt + l.

You will find a console.log that produces a log message in the format of:

TCL: functionName -> variableName, variableValue

Additionally, you can comment on all console.log with the press of a button.

MATERIAL THEME FOR VISUAL STUDIO CODE

It is one of the most popular themes, and versions are created for various IDEs and code editors such as IntelliJ, Atom, Sublime, and VS Code. It is delightful and thoroughly satisfying to work with and comes in multiple variants for all editors.

It's delightful and satisfying to work with and comes in different color variants for all tastes.

This theme is available in almost every IDE such as Nova, iTerm, Bear notes, and NetBeans.

Installation

You can install the material theme in any of the operating systems:

- Linux Ctrl + P

- macOS ⌘P

- Windows Ctrl + P

Run the following command and press Enter:
ext install material theme
Activate material theme for your local operating system:

- Linux Ctrl + Shift + P

- MacOS ⌘ + Shift + P

- Windows Ctrl + Shift + P

Type "theme" in the Command Palette, choose Preferences: Color Theme, and select any of the Material Theme variants from the list. After activation of the extension, the theme will set the correct icon theme.

Set the accent color

- Linux Ctrl + Shift + P

- MacOS ⌘ + Shift + P

- Windows Ctrl + Shift + P

Type "material theme" in the Command Palette, choose Material Theme. Set accent color and select one of the Material Theme variants from the list.

To customize the themes, you can use color scheme changes. You can set the light, dark, and high contrast themes with the settings:

- **workbench.preferredLightColorTheme:** set defaults to "Default Light+"

- **workbench.preferredDarkColorTheme:** set defaults to "Default Dark+"

- **workbench.preferredHighContrastColorTheme:** set defaults to "Default High Contrast"

Theme Color

Open the Color Theme picker through file> Preferences > Color Theme or Code > Preferences > Color Theme on macOS. (keyboard shortcut Ctrl + K Ctrl + T) to display the selector, select the theme you want, and press Enter to activate the color theme in your user settings (keyboard shortcut Ctrl + ,).

```
// It specifies the color theme used in the workbench.
"workbench.colorTheme" : "Default Dark+"
```

Color Formats

Color values are defined in the RGB color model with an alpha channel for transparency. The following hexadecimal examples are supported: #RGB where R is (red), G is (green), B is (blue), and A is (alpha). This three-digit notation is a shorter version of the six-digit form #RRGGBBAA, and the four-digit RGB notation #RGBA is a shorter version of the eight-digit form #RRGGBB and are hexadecimal characters (0-9, a-f or A-F).\

If the alpha value is not defined, it defaults to an opaque FF value, with no transparency. When alpha is set to 00, the color is fully transparent.

Base Colors in the Material Theme

- **focusBorder:** It is the overall border color for focused elements, and this color will be used if another component does not override it.

- **Foreground:** It is the overall foreground color. This color will be used if another component does not override it.

- **Widget.shadow:** It is used as the Shadow color of widgets such as Find/Replace inside the code editor.

- **selection.background:** It set the background color of text selections in the workbench.

- **descriptionForeground:** Foreground color for description text providing additional information.

- **icon.foreground:** It is the default color for icons in the workbench.

- **sash.hoverBorder:** It is hover border color for draggable sashes.

Workbench Colors in the Material Theme

You can change your color theme using the workbench.colorCustomizations, and editor.tokenColorCustomizations in user settings.

To set the colors of User Interface elements such as list & trees, widget, diff editor, activity bar, notifications, scroll bar, split view, buttons, and more, using workbench.colorCustomizations.

Some Features Material Theme

- Have a curated color palette.

- Five various theme variants.

- Different file and folders icons.

- Free from distractions.

- Available for many tools.

- Provides you with constant updates.

Try out this extension the link is given below:
https://marketplace.visualstudio.com/items?itemName=Equinusocio
.vsc-material-theme

AUTOPREFIXER FOR VISUAL STUDIO CODE

Installation

- **Press F1 and select Extensions:** Install Extensions.

- Search and choose vscode-autoprefixer.

Use can press F1 and run the command Autoprefixer: Run.

Languages Supported by Autoprefixer

- CSS

- Less

- SCSS

Supported Settings

- autoprefixer.findExternalAutoprefixer, type is Boolean, and the default value is false.

- autoprefixer. options, type is Object, and the default value is false.

- autoprefixer.formatOnSave, type is Boolean, and the default value is false.

- autoprefixer. options, type is Object, and the default value is false.

- autoprefixer.ignoreFiles, type is Array and default value is [].

- autoprefixer.findExternalAutoprefixer, type is Boolean, and the default value is false.

You can install Autoprefixer using npm package:

- npm I –D autoprefixer

- npm I –g autoprefixer

EsLint on VS Code with Airbnb Javascript Style

It is a collection of standards that describe how JavaScript should be written. There are many popular JavaScript style guides.

Lint or linter is a tool that analyzes code to flag stylistic errors, errors, bugs, and suspicious constructs. In contrast, EsLint is a pluggable and configurable linter tool for identifying and reporting patterns in JavaScript and helps maintain your code quality with ease.

Download Node.js and install it. Node.js comes under a package manager called npm, which we'll use in setting up EsLint.

Create a folder for your project.

After installing Node.js, create a new directory and open it:

- mkdir folder_name

- cd folder_name

Now initialize a new npm config in the root directory:

npm init –yes

Installing EsLint and Airbnb Packages

npm install eslint eslint-config-Airbnb-base eslint-plugin-import –d

The extension uses the ESLint library in the workspace. If you have not installed ESLint either locally or globally by running npm, install eslint in the workspace folder for a local install or npm install -g eslint for a global install.

TERMINAL FOR VISUAL STUDIO CODE

It is used to run the terminal commands directly in the code editor for a particular folder. You need not open the command prompt separately.

But it includes some key points to speed up things a little more; check out these features:

- It runs all the commands in Text Editor.

- It runs the selected commands in Text Editor.

- It stops the running commands.

- You can easily view output in Output Window.

- It opens an integrated terminal at the current file directory.

- A quick way to toggle Integrated Terminal Command.

PATH INTELLISENSE FOR VISUAL STUDIO CODE

It is a code-completion plug-in that includes several features like List Members, Parameter Info, Quick Info, and Complete Word. These features help you learn more about the code when using it, keep track of the parameters, and add calls to properties and methods with a few keystrokes.

In the Command Palette (Ctrl + Shift + P), select Install Extension and choose Path IntelliSense if you have installed it; otherwise, download the Path IntelliSense from the Marketplace.

To use Path IntelliSense, the following configuration option must be added to your settings:

```
{ "typescript.suggest.paths": false }
{ "javascript.suggest.paths": false }
```

Settings

File Extension in Import Statements

Path IntelliSense will remove the files extension by default if the statement is an import statement. To enable this files extension set the following setting as true:

```
{
  "path-intellisense.extensionOnImport": true,
}
```

Show Hidden Files

To show the hidden files, set the configuration to show hidden files to true:

```
{
  "path-intellisense.showHiddenFiles": true,
}
```

Auto Slash When Navigating to Folders

By default, the auto-completion does not add a slash after a directory.

```
{
  "path-intellisense.autoSlashAfterDirectory": false,
}
```

Absolute Paths

By default, absolute paths are displayed within the current workspace root path. Set it to false to set absolute paths to the disk root path.

```
{
  "path-intellisense.absolutePathToWorkspace": true,
}
```

npm Intellisense

In the Command Palette (Ctrl + Shift + P) select Install Extension and choose npm Intellisense.

The npm extension provides you with two features:

1. running npm scripts defined in the package.json in the editor

2. validating the packages listed in the package.json.

The npm IntelliSense extension introduces some autocomplete behavior when you need to import modules into your code.

Scan devDependencies

npm IntelliSense will scan only dependencies by default. Set the scanDevDependencies to true to enable it for devDependencies too.

```
{
  "npm-intellisense.scanDevDependencies": true,
}
```

Show Built-In (local) libs

It shows build-in node modules like "path" of "fs".

```
{
  "npm-intellisense.showBuildInLibs": true,
}
```

It lookup package.json for recursive

It looks for package.json inside the nearest directory instead of the workspace root directory. It's enabled by default.

```
{
  "npm-intellisense.recursivePackageJsonLookup":
  true,
}
```

Package Subfolder IntelliSense

It opens the subfolders of a module. This feature is only for work in progress and experiments.

```
{
  "npm-intellisense.packageSubfoldersIntellisense":
  false,
}
```

TABNINE FOR VISUAL STUDIO CODE

What Is Tabnine?

It is next-level productivity for professional teams and developers. It is a tool for AI code completion trusted by millions of developers to amplify coding accuracy and boost productivity. You code faster with lesser errors. Whether you are a beginner developer or a seasoned pro, working solo or part of a team, Tabnine will help you push your productivity to new heights, all in your favorite IDE.

Tabnine AI Assistant and AI Engine

You call it IntelliJ Code, IntelliSense, autocomplete, AI-powered code completion, AI-assisted code completion, AI copilot, code suggestion, AI code snippets, code prediction, code hinting, or content assist, and you already know that it can save you tons of time.

It is powered by machine learning models trained on billions of trusted open-source code lines from GitHub. It is the most advanced AI-powered code completion copilot. And like GitHub, it is also an essential tool for professional developers.

It delivers three times more AI for better collaboration, better privacy protection, and better code completion.

Here is the link to Tabnine: https://marketplace.visualstudio.com/items?itemName=TabNine.tabnine-vscode

All the languages supported include:

- Python
- JavaScript
- extended JS
- Java
- C/C++/C#
- React
- PHP
- Go
- CSharp
- Ruby
- C Header
- Objective-C
- Rust
- Swift
- Typescript
- Haskell
- ML
- F#

- Scala

- Kotlin

- Perl

- SQL

- Shell

- JSON

- YAML

- TOM

- HTML

- CSS

- Julia

- Markdown

- Lua

- Dart

- Vue

- Bash

Key Features

- Speed up your development.

- Team learning algorithm.

- Provide privacy and protection.

- The ultimate AI assistant.

- Easy and secure GitHub integration.

- It makes it easy and secure for Pro users to grant their AI assistant read-access to the GitHub repositories.

- Reduce development costs.

- Best open-source coding practices from across the globe.

- Get quick, concise code suggestions.

CodeStream

CodeStream is a developer collaboration platform that combines essential dev tools into VS Code. It eliminates context-switching and simplifies code discussion and code review by putting all tools in your single IDE.

Integrations in Codestream

- Code Hosts such as GitHub, GitHub Enterprise,Bitbucket, Bitbucket Server, GitLab, GitLab Self-Managed

- Issue Trackers such as Azure DevOps, Bitbucket, Asana, Clubhouse, GitHub, GitLab, GitLab Self-Managed, GitHub Enterprise, Jira, Linear, Trello, YouTrack

- Observability: New Relic One, Pixie

- Messaging Services such as Slack, Microsoft Teams

Requirements

- It requires the latest version of Visual Studio Code and is also available for JetBrains or Visual Studio.

- Your repository has to be managed by Git or a Git-hosting service like GitHub.

JUPYTER EXTENSION FOR VISUAL STUDIO CODE

It is an extension of Visual Studio Code Marketplace that provides essential notebook support for language kernels supported in Jupyter Notebooks. Many kernels will work with no modification to enable the advanced features. It includes the Jupyter Keymaps and the Jupyter Notebook Renderers extensions by default. Also, it provides Jupyter-consistent keymaps and the Jupyter Notebook Renderers extension for mime types such as latex, vega, plotly, and the like. Both can be disabled as well as uninstalled.

Working with Other Languages

The Jupyter can support other languages in addition to Python such as Julia, R, and C# in VS Code Insiders with the latest Native VS Code Notebooks Experience!

Quick Installation

- Install VS Code Insiders.

- If it is not working with Python, make sure that you have a Jupyter kernelspec corresponding to the language you would like to use installed on your machine.

- Install the Jupyter extension.

- Open or create a new notebook file and start coding.

Useful Commands in Jupyter

Open the Command Palette or Ctrl + Shift + P on macOS and Ctrl + Shift + P on Windows/Linux and type in any of the following commands:

Command	Description
Jupyter: Create New Blank Notebook	It creates a new blank Jupyter Notebook.
Notebook: Select Notebook Kernel	It selects or switches kernels within your notebook.
Notebook: Change Cell Language	It changes the language of the cell.
Jupyter: Export to HTML Jupyter: Export to PDF.	It creates a presentation-friendly version of your notebook in HTML or PDF.

Supported Locales

The extension is available in multiple languages:

- ko-ko

- nl

- de

- en

- es

- fa

- fr

- it

- ja

- pl

- pt-br

- ru

- tr

- zh-en

- zh-TW

Jupyter Notebook Quick Start

- To create a new notebook, open the Command Palette. In Windows, use Ctrl + Shift + P, and in macOS: Command + Shift + P, select the "Jupyter: Create New Blank Notebook".

- Select your kernel by clicking on the selector in the top right corner of the notebook or by calling the "Notebook: Select Notebook Kernel" command.

- To change the language click the language picker or call the "Notebook: Change Cell Language" command.

Features Support

- Many editor extensions like VIM, linters, bracket colorization, and many more are available while editing a cell.

- It supports VS Code's vast array of basic code editing features like find and replace, hot exit, and code folding.

- Deep integration with workbench and file-based features in VS Code like the table of content, breadcrumbs, and additional operations.

- It loads quickly for Jupyter notebook (.ipynb) files.

- The file is loaded and rendered as quickly as possible in Jupyter.

- Including a notebook-friendly diff tool, you are making it much easier to compare between code cells.

- Provides extensibility beyond what the Jupyter extension is.

- Extensions can now add their language or runtime-specific take on notebooks, like the .NET Interactive Notebooks and Gather.

- The Jupyter extension comes under the packages with a large set of the most commonly used renderers for output.

PLACE

It is fast, full of rich features, and language support for Python.

It is an extension that can work with Python in Visual Studio Code to provide better language support, and Pyright powers it. Using Pyright, the Pylance extension can supercharge your Python IntelliSense experience with rich information that helps you write better code faster. The place is the default language for Python in Visual Studio Code. It is shipped as part of that extension as an optional dependency.

Installation

- Install the Python extension from the VS Code Marketplace. It will be installed as an optional extension.

- Open any Python (.py) file, and the Pylance extension will activate.

Place excellent features for Python 3, including:

- It provides docstrings

- Is Signature help, with type information

- Show parameter suggestions

- Supporting code completion

- It provides auto-imports with add and removes import code actions features

- Reporting of code errors and warnings

- Code outline

- Code navigation

- Type checking mode

- Native multi-root workspace support

- IntelliCode compatibility

- Jupyter Notebooks compatibility

- Semantic highlighting

MAVEN FOR JAVA EXTENSION

Maven extension is for code editor. It provides a project explorer and various shortcuts to execute Maven commands in command prompt or within the project, or improving the user experience for Java developers who use Maven.

It is a project management tool that is based on POM (project object model). It is used to build projects, dependencies, and documentation.

There are various problems that we will face during the project development in Maven. They might be:

- **Adding collections of Jars in each project:** In the case of spring, struts, and hibernate frameworks, we need to set of jar files in each project by adding them. It should be including all the dependencies of jars.

- Creating the correct project structure, then we must need to create the right structure in struts, servlet etc., otherwise it will not execute in any way.

- For building and deploying the project, then we need to build and deploy the project so that it may work.

What Maven does?

It simplifies the mentioned problems. It does mainly the following tasks:

- Makes a project easy to build and development.

- Provides a uniform build process and it is shared by all the Maven projects.

- Provides you a project's information such as log document, sources, mailing list, dependency list, cross-referenced, unit test reports, etc.

- It also helps to manage some attributes such as documentation, builds, reporting, scams, releases, distribution, etc.

Features

- It supports generating projects from Maven Archetype.

- It supports generating effective POM.

- It provides shortcuts to common goals, plug-in goals, and customized commands.

- It preserves command history to fast re-run.

Requirements

- Java

- Maven/Maven Wrapper

Basic Usage

- Maven Explorer

- Run Plug-in Goals

- POM File Editing

- Re-Run Historical Commands

- Archetype Related

Additional Configurations

- JAVA_HOME and Other Environment Variables

  It executes Maven by opening a terminal and then calling Maven in that specific session. It requires the JAVA_HOME environment variable to be set. It will look for other variables like MAVEN_OPTS.

  If you have not set variables permanently, you can also configure them, or set any other environment variable in the settings.

- Special Handling for JAVA_HOME

  With this, you can easily specify JAVA_HOME in a place, and you do not need to use the maven.terminal.customEnv setting unless you have other environment variables to set.

  If you have JAVA_HOME configured using the maven.terminal. customEnv setting, and also have specified to reuse the Red Hat setting, then the value from maven.terminal.customEnv will take as precedence.

- Default Options for Maven Command

The usage of Maven executable will be –

Usage: mvn [options] [<goal(s)>] [<phase(s)>]

You can also use maven.executable.options to define the default options for all your Maven commands executed in the currently active project.

- Folder Exclusion for Searching POM Files

  To speed up things like searching of Maven projects, you can exclude folders in settings:

```
{
 "maven.excludedFolders": [
 "**/.*",    // It excludes hidden folders
 "**/node_modules",  // It excludes node modules to
speed up
 "**/target"   // It excludes duplicated pom file
in target folder
 ]
}
```

- Customize Favorite Maven Commands

Name	Description	Default Value
Name	Description	Default Value
maven.excludedFolders	It specifies the file path pattern of folders to exclude while searching for Maven projects.	It's default value is ["**/.*", "**/node_modules", "**/target", "**/bin", "**/archetype-resources"]
maven.executable. preferMavenWrapper	It specifies you prefer to use a Maven wrapper. When true, it tries using "mvnw" by walking up the parent folders, or when false, "mvnw" is not found, it tries "mvn" in PATH instead.	true
maven.executable.path	It specifies absolute path of "mvn" executable. When this value is empty, it tries using "mvn" or "mvnw" according to the value of "maven.executable. preferMavenWrapper." E.g., /usr/ local/apache-maven-3.6.0/bin/mvn	

(Continued)

Name	Description	Default Value
maven.executable.options Specifies default options for all mvn commands. E.g., -o -DskipTests		
maven.projectOpenBehavior Default method of opening newly created project. "Interactive"		
maven.pomfile.globPattern It specifies the glob pattern used to look for pom.xml files. **/pom.xml		
maven.pomfile. autoUpdateEffectivePOM It specifies whether to update effective POM automatically whenever changes detected. false		
maven.terminal.customEnv It specifies an array of variable names and values. These variable values will be added before Maven is executed.		
maven.terminal.favorites It specifies pre-defined favorite commands to execute. alias: It is the short name for the command. command: Content of the favorite command. []		
maven.view It specifies the way of viewing Maven projects. Possible values: flat, hierarchical. flat		
maven.settingsFile Specifies the absolute path of the Maven settings.xml file. If not specified, ~/.m2/settings.XML is used. null		
environmentVariable:It is the name of the environment variable to set. value: Value of the environment variable to set. []		
maven.terminal.useJavaHome When a value is true, and if the setting java.home has a value, then the environment variable JAVA_HOME will be set to the value of java.home when a new terminal window is created. false		

Here is the link to Maven for Java extension:

https://marketplace.visualstudio.com/items?itemName=vscjava.
vscode-maven&ssr=false#review-details

LANGUAGE SUPPORT FOR JAVA FOR VS CODE
Installation of Language Support for Java

- **Install the extension from the below link:** https://marketplace.visu-alstudio.com/items?itemName=redhat.java

- If you don't have a Java Development Kit (JDK), correctly set then download and install the latest Java Development Kit (Java 11 with the minimum requirement).

- The extension is activated when you first access a Java file; it recognizes projects with Maven or Gradle build files in the directory hierarchy.

Some Features

- It supports code from Java 1.5 to the latest.

- It supports Maven pom.xml project.

- It supports basic Gradle Java project (Android not supported).

- It supports standalone Java files.

- While typing reporting of parsing and compilation errors.

- Support code completion (IntelliSense).

- Support code, source actions, and refactoring.

- Javadoc hovers.

- It organize importing statements.

- Triggers manually on save.

- When pasting code into a Java file with Ctrl + Shift + V (Cmd + Shift +v on Mac).

- Code folding.

- Code navigation.

- Type search.

- Code outline.

- Semantic selection.

- Diagnostic tags.

- Code lens (references/implementations).

- Support highlights.

- Code formatting (on-type/selection/file).

- Code snippets.

- Annotation processing support (automatic for Maven projects).

- Call hierarchy.

- Type hierarchy.

Java Tooling JDK

JDK will be used to launch the Java Language Server. And by default will be used to compile your projects.

The path to the JDK can be specified by the java.home setting in VS Code workspace or user settings. If it is not specified, it is searched in the following order until a JDK meets the current requirement

- on the current system path

- the JDK_HOME environment variable

- the JAVA_HOME environment variable

Java commands

Command	Description
Switch to standard mode	It switches the Java Language Server to standard mode. This command is available when the Java Language Server is in lightweight mode.
Java: Update Project (Shift + Alt + U)	It is available when the editor is focused on a Maven pom.xml or a Gradle file. It forces project configuration/classpath updates.
Java: Import Java Projects into workspace	It detects and imports all the Java projects into the Java Language Server workspace.

(Continued)

Command	Description
Java: Open Java Language Server Log File	It opens the Java Language Server log file, useful for troubleshooting problems.
Java: Remove Folder from Java Source Path	It removes the selected folder from its project source path. This command is only available in the file explorer context menu and only works for unmanaged folders.
Java: Open Java Extension Log File	It opens the Java extension log file, useful for troubleshooting problems.
Java: Open All Log Files	It opens both the Java Language Server log file and the Java extension log file.
Java: List All Java Source Paths	It lists all the Java source paths recognized by the Java Language Server workspace.
Java: Force Java Compilation (Shift + Alt + B)	It manually triggers the compilation of the workspace.

Java Supported VS Code Settings

Command	Description
java.home	It gives an absolute path to the JDK home folder used to launch the Java Language Server. Requires VS Code restart.
java.jdt.ls.vmargs	It provides extra VM arguments used to launch the Java Language Server. Requires VS Code restart.
java.errors.incompleteClasspath.severity	It specifies the severity of the message when the classpath is incomplete for a Java file. Supported values are ignore, info, warning, error.
java.trace.server	It traces the communication between VS Code and the Java Language Server.
ava.configuration.updateBuildConfig uration	It specifies how modifications on build files update the Java classpath/configuration.
java.configuration.checkProjectSettingsE xclusions:	It controls whether to exclude extension-generated project settings files
java.implementationsCodeLens.enabled	It enable/disable the implementations code lenses.
java.import.gradle.enabled	It enables/disables the Gradle importer.
java.referencesCodeLens.enabled	It enable/disable the references code lenses.
java.import.gradle.jvmArguments	It is JVM arguments to pass to Gradle.
java.autobuild.enabled	It enable/disable the auto build
java.import.gradle.arguments	The arguments to pass to Gradle.
java.maxConcurrentBuilds	It sets max simultaneous project builds.
java.configuration.maven.userSettings	It is path to Maven's user settings.xml file.

Semantic Highlighting

It fixes syntax highlighting issues with the default Java Textmate grammar. You might experience a few minor issues. It can be disabled for all languages using the editor.semanticHighlighting.enabled setting, or for Java using language-specific editor settings.

BEAUTIFY JAVASCRIPT, JSON, CSS, SASS, AND HTML EXTENSION FOR VS CODE

VS Code editor uses js-beautify internally, but it lacks the ability to modify the style you like to use. This extension enables running js-beautify in VS Code and honoring any .jsbeautifyrc file in the open file path tree to load your code styling. Run with F1 Beautify (to beautify a selection) or F1 Beautify file. The .jsbeautifyrc configuration parser accepts sub-elements of HTML, js, and CSS so it can be used for each of the beautifiers.

Note: This will cause the configuration file to be incorrectly structured for running js-beautify from the command line.

Some jsbeautifyrc setting are eol, tab_size, indent_with_tabs, wrap_line_length.wrap_attributes,unformatted,indent_inner_html,indent_handlebars,end_with_newline,pace_after_anon_function,space_in_paren etc.

VISUAL STUDIO INTELLICODE FOR VISUAL STUDIO CODE

This extension provides AI-assisted development features for TypeScript/JavaScript, Python, and for Java developers in Visual Studio Code, and insights based on understanding your code context combined with machine learning.

You will need Visual Studio Code version 1.29.1 or later to use this extension. For each supported language, please go to the "Getting Started" section below to understand any other requirement you will need to install and configure to get IntelliCode completions.

About IntelliCode

This provides AI-assisted IntelliSense by showing recommended completion items for your code context at the top of the completions list. The IntelliCode extension provides AI-assisted IntelliSense for Python, JavaScript. Java, and TypeScript.

Install the Visual Studio IntelliCode extension by clicking the install link on: https://marketplace.visualstudio.com/items?itemName=VisualStudioExptTeam.vscodeintellicode

The supported languages for AI-assisted IntelliSense are:

- Python
- SQL
- Java
- JavaScript and TypeScript
- C#
- XAML
- C++
- Visual Basic

Workloads

It was included in Visual Studio 2019 version 16.4 as part of any of the following workloads:

- .NET Core cross-platform development
- ASP.NET and web development
- Azure development
- .NET desktop development
- Mobile development with .NET
- Game development with Unity
- Visual Studio extension development
- Universal Windows Platform development
- Office/SharePoint development
- Desktop development with C++
- Game development with C++
- Mobile development with C++
- Linux development with C++

VS Code JSHint Extension

Environment Setup

It looks for a JSHint module in the root directory and in the global package location. You can install JSHint locally or globally using npm install -g jshint (g means global). If your module is in a different location, use the jshint.nodePath setting to specify the path. The jshint.packageManager setting can be used to specify which package manager you are using – npm or yarn.

Install the Visual Studio IntelliCode extension by clicking the install link on: https://marketplace.visualstudio.com/items?itemName =dbaeumer.jshint

Configuration

Uses the standard JSHint configuration options described on the JSHint website.

Installation

It runs in a number of different environments; installation is different for each.

Browser-Like Environments

A standalone file is built for browser-like environments with every release. You will find it in the dist directory of the download.

VS Code JSHint Installation Using Node.js

You can install it globally by the following command:

```
npm install -g jshint
```

After this installation, you can use the JSHint command-line interface.

It is easy to install JSHint as a development dependency within an existing Node.js project:

```
npm install - save-dev jshint
```

Plug-Ins for Text Editor and Various IDEs

For Sublime Text:

- Sublime-JSHint Gutter plug-in for graphically displaying lint results in ST2 and ST3.

- Sublime-jshint plug-in for build package for ST2.
- Sublime Linter plug-in for lint highlighting for ST2.

For Atom

- JSHint for Atom, JSHint package for Atom.
- linter-jshint, JSHint plug-in for Atom's Linter.

For TextMate

- JSLintMate (supports both JSHint and JSLint)
- JSHint-external TextMate Bundle
- JSHint Bundle for TextMate 2
- JSHint TextMate Bundle

For Visual Studio

- SharpLinter (supports both JSLint and JSHint).
- JSLint for Visual Studio (supports both JSLint and JSHint).
- Web Essentials (Runs JSHint automatically).

For Visual Studio Code

- VS Code JSHint extension, integrates JSHint into VS Code.

Brackets

- Brackets Interactive Linter
- Brackets JSHint plug-in

Extra plugins for other editors

- JSLint out of the box.
- JSLint plug-in for Notepad++ now supports JSHint.

- **JSHint integration:** It is for the NetBeans IDE

- JetBrains IDE family supports realtime code inspection with both JSHint and

- JSHint plug-in for Gedit.

- ShiftEdit IDE has built-in support for JSHint.

- Komodo 7 presently ships with built-in support for JSHint.

- JSHint integration is for the Eclipse IDE.

- **JSXHint:** It is a wrapper around JSHint to allow the linting of files containing JSX syntax.

- **JSHintr:** It is a web tool that allows you to set your own code standards, easily review a file against these standards, and share the output with other developers.

- **FixMyJS:** It is a tool that automatically fixes mistakes – such as missing semicolons, multiple definitions, etc. – reported by JSHint.

- **overcommit:** It is an extensible Git hook manager with built-in JSHint linting, distributed as a Ruby gem. Read more about it.

- **QHint:** JSHint in QUnit – It check for errors in your code from within your unit tests. Lint errors result in failed tests.

KUBERNETES

It is for developers building applications to run in Kubernetes clusters and for DevOps staff troubleshooting Kubernetes applications.

Features include:

- It view your clusters in an explorer tree view, and drills them into pods, nodes.workloads, and services.

- It browses Helm repos and install charts into the Kubernetes cluster.

- Provides IntelliSense for Kubernetes resources, Helm charts, and templates.

- It helps to edit Kubernetes resource manifests and apply them to cluster.

- It is used to build and run containers in your cluster from Dockerfiles in your project.

- It views the diffs of a resource's current state against the resource manifest in the Git repository.

- It can easily check out the Git commit corresponding to a deployed application.

- It runs commands or starts a shell within application pods.

- It gets or follows logs and events from any clusters.

Installation

Install the Kubernetes extension by clicking the install link on: https://marketplace.visualstudio.com/items?itemName=ms-kubernetes-tools.vscode-kubernetes-tools

Dependencies

This extension may need to invoke the following command-line tools, depending on which features you are using. You will need kubectl at minimum and Docker or buildah if you wish to use the extension to build applications rather than only browse.

- kubectl

- Docker or buildah

- helm

Commands for Kubernetes

- **Kubernetes: Load:** It loads a resource from the Kubernetes API and creates a new editor window.

- **Kubernetes: Get:** It gets the status for a specific resource.

- **Kubernetes: Logs:** It opens a view with a set of options to display/follow logs.

- **Kubernetes: Follow Events:** It follows events on a selected namespace.

- **Kubernetes: Show Events:** It shows events on a selected namespace.

- **Kubernetes: Watch:** It watches a specific resource or all resources of that object type and updates the cluster explorer as they change.

- **Kubernetes: Stop Watching:** It stops watching the specific resource.

REMOTE DEVELOPMENT EXTENSION PACK FOR VISUAL STUDIO CODE

This extension pack allows us to open any folder in a container, on a remote machine, in the Windows Subsystem for Linux (WSL).

- You can develop on the same operating system you deploy and it is faster hardware than your local machine.

- It helps new members/contributors get more productive quickly.

- It takes advantage of a Linux-based tool-chain.

This extension pack includes three extensions:

1. **Remote:** SSH

2. **Remote:** Containers

3. **Remote:** WSL

Installation

Install VS Code or VS Code Insiders (just a beta version includes the latest features and bug fixes, but new features may or may not be stable) and this extension pack too. On Windows, be sure to check to Add to PATH while installing.

- **For Remote:** SSH, install an OpenSSH compatible SSH client.

- **For Remote:** WSL, Install the Windows Subsystem for Linux along with your preferred Linux distribution.

- **For Remote:** Containers, Install and configure Docker for your operating system.

For Windows or macOS

- Install Docker Desktop latest version in Mac/Windows.

- If not have WSL2 on Windows, right-click on the Docker taskbar, select Settings/Preferences, and update Resources > File Sharing with any locations your source code is kept.

- To enable the Windows WSL2 back-end, right-click on the Docker taskbar item and select Settings. Check use the WSL2-based engine and verify your distribution is enabled under Resources > WSL Integration.

Linux

Follow the installation instructions for Docker. I use Docker Compose, follow the Docker Compose installation instructions.

Add user to the Docker group by using a terminal to run: sudo usermod -aG docker $USER. Sign out and back in again so this setting takes effect.

CHAPTER SUMMARY

In this chapter, we have discussed VS Code extensions and looked at some commonly used extensions that help you to enhance your coding experience with their features.

Appraisal

VS CODE WAS FIRST announced on April 29, 2015, and its source code was officially released under the MIT license and made available on GitHub. Visual Studio Code is the first cross-platform, multi-language development tool in the Microsoft Visual Studio family that runs on Windows, Linux, and Mac OS X. It is free and open source. It is a code-centric tool, which makes it easier to edit code files and folder-based project systems and write cross-platform web and mobile applications for the most popular platforms, such as Node.js and the new ASP.NET Core. It is a prevalent and influential code-focused development environment mainly designed to make coding easier to write web, mobile, and cloud applications using languages that are available to different development platforms and to support the application development lifecycle with a built-in debugger and with integrated support to the popular Git version control engine. It has integrated support for many languages and rich editing features such as IntelliSense, finding symbol references, quickly reaching a type definition, and much more. Its main aims are to provide a developer with the tools for quick coding and leave a more complex workflow to fuller featured IDEs. This is an essential investment from Microsoft, representing another significant step in Redmond's new "open" way of thinking.

Visual Studio Code combines the simplicity of a powerful code editor with the tools a developer needs to support the application life-cycle development, including debuggers and Git version control integration. As a result, rather than being a basic code editor, it is a comprehensive development tool. Visual Studio 2015 is clearly the better choice for more complex coding and development – remember that the Community edition is free – but Visual Studio Code may be useful in a variety of circumstances. It is a source code editor that can be used with various programming languages, including Java, Go, and Python.

Before you continue reading, make sure you have installed the correct version of Visual Studio Code. Installers are available for Mac OS X, Linux, and Windows. You can follow the official documentation in case you have trouble installing the software. Microsoft is releasing new versions of Visual Studio Code very frequently, typically once a month. The environment periodically checks for further updates and, when available, prompts you to install the new release and then asks to be restarted when finished. This book has been written using version1.6.0.

For this reason, some features might have changed at the time of your reading, others might have been improved, and others might be new. This is a necessary clarification that you should keep in mind while reading, and this is also why we often provide links to the official documentation. Interestingly, there is also a Visual Studio Code – Insiders build that works side by side with the regular release and automatically installs updates on your behalf. If you are interested, remember that this is a separate installation, which implies installing extensions and configuring settings separately.

In this book, you will learn how to use and get the most out of Visual Studio Code, seeing how you can use it both as a powerful code editor and a complete environment for end-to-end development. The figures are based on the Microsoft Windows 10 operating system, although Linux and Mac OS X users will see no difference. Also, Visual Studio Code includes several color themes that style its layout. I'm using the so-called Light Theme so that you might see different colors than I, but, again, the colors you use certainly do not affect what we have explained here. We have also explained how to change the color theme, but if you are impatient or want to be consistent with the book's figures, select File > Preferences > Colour Theme.

Now sit down, open Visual Studio Code, and enjoy this fantastic tool. We are sure you'll love it.

Bibliography

anandmeg. (2022, June 7). *Install Visual Studio | Microsoft Docs*. https://docs
.microsoft.com/en-us/visualstudio/install/install-visual-studio?view=vs
-2022

Auto Rename Tag. (2001, August 1). Visual Studio Marketplace. https://market-
place.visualstudio.com/items?itemName=formulahendry.auto-rename-tag

Autoprefixer. (2001, March 1). Visual Studio Marketplace. https://marketplace.
visualstudio.com/items?itemName=mrmlnc.vscode-autoprefixer

Basic Editing in Visual Studio Code. (n.d.). Retrieved July 9, 2022, from https://
code.visualstudio.com/docs/editor/codebasics#:~:text=VS%20Code
%20allows%20you%20to%20quickly%20search%20over%20all%20files,
each%20file%20and%20its%20location

Beautify. (2001, March 1). Visual Studio Marketplace. https://marketplace.visual-
studio.com/items?itemName=HookyQR.beautify

Bracket Pair Colorization Toggler. (2001, February 1). Visual Studio Marketplace.
https://marketplace.visualstudio.com/items?itemName=dzhavat.bracket
-pair-toggler

CodeSnap. (2001, March 1). Visual Studio Marketplace. https://marketplace.visu-
alstudio.com/items?itemName=adpyke.codesnap

Color Highlight. (2001, March 1). Visual Studio Marketplace. https://marketplace
.visualstudio.com/items?itemName=naumovs.color-highlight

Copes, F. (2018, May 31). *A Visual Studio Code Tutorial*. https://flaviocopes.com
/vscode/#:~:text=The%20code%20of%20the%20editor,for%20all%20us
%20JavaScript%20developers

CSS Peek. (2001, September 1). Visual Studio Marketplace. https://marketplace
.visualstudio.com/items?itemName=pranaygp.vscode-css-peek

CSS, SCSS, and Less Support in Visual Studio Code. (n.d.). Retrieved July 9, 2022,
from https://code.visualstudio.com/docs/languages/css

Debug Node.js Apps using Visual Studio Code. (n.d.). Retrieved July 9, 2022, from
https://code.visualstudio.com/docs/nodejs/nodejs-debugging

Debugger Extension. (n.d.). Visual Studio Code ExtensionAPI. Retrieved July
9, 2022, from https://code.visualstudio.com/api/extension-guides/debug-
ger-extension#:~:text=Visual%20Studio%20Code's%20debugging%20arc
hitecture,interface%20with%20all%20of%20them.&text=This%20screens
hot%20shows%20the%20following,Debug%20configuration%20manage
ment

Debugging in Visual Studio Code. (n.d.). Retrieved July 9, 2022, from https://code
.visualstudio.com/docs/editor/debugging#:~:text=Debugger%20extensions
%23,that%20gets%20transpiled%20to%20JavaScript

[Deprecated] Debugger for Chrome. (2001, March 1). Visual Studio Marketplace.
https://marketplace.visualstudio.com/items?itemName=msjsdiag.debug-
ger-for-chrome

Difference between IDE and Text Editor | Difference between. (2020, October
24). http://www.differencebetween.net/technology/difference-between-ide
-and-text-editor/#:~:text=full%2Dfeatured%20IDE.-,A%20text%20editor
%20is%20simply%20a%20computer%20program%20and%20a,to%20build
%20and%20test%20software

Documentation for Visual Studio Code. (n.d.). Retrieved July 9, 2022, from https://
code.visualstudio.com/docs

Extension API. (n.d.). Visual Studio Code ExtensionAPI. Retrieved July 9, 2022,
from https://code.visualstudio.com/api

Gehman, C. (n.d.). *What is Source Control and Why is it Important?* Perforce
Software. Retrieved July 9, 2022, from https://www.perforce.com/blog/vcs/
what-source-control

Get Started Tutorial for Python in Visual Studio Code. (n.d.). Retrieved July 9,
2022, from https://code.visualstudio.com/docs/python/python-tutorial

GitLens — Git Supercharged. (2001, September 1). Visual Studio Marketplace.
https://marketplace.visualstudio.com/items?itemName=eamodio.gitlens

Goyal, Y. (n.d.). *MonoDevelop vs Visual Studio.* Retrieved July 9, 2022, from
https://www.educba.com/monodevelop-vs-visual-studio/

Gupta, R. (2020, July 22). *Visual Studio Code (VS Code) Integration with Git
Source Control.* SQL Shack - Articles about Database Auditing, Server
Performance, Data Recovery, and More. https://www.sqlshack.com/visual
-studio-code-vs-code-integration-with-git-source-control/#:~:text=VS
%20code%20contains%20integrated%20Git,Open%20Folder%20and
%20Clone%20Repository

Hicks, S. (2021, May 21). *Sublime Text vs VSCode Which Editor Should You Use
for Software Development.* Tangent Technologies. https://tangenttechnolo-
gies.ca/blog/sublime-text-vs-vscode/#:~:text=Sublime%20Text%20and
%20Visual%20Studio,on%20Windows%2C%20Mac%20and%20Linux

HTML Programming with Visual Studio Code. (n.d.). Retrieved July 9, 2022, from
https://code.visualstudio.com/docs/languages/html

indent-rainbow. (2001, March 1). Visual Studio Marketplace. https://marketplace
.visualstudio.com/items?itemName=oderwat.indent-rainbow

IntelliSense in Visual Studio Code. (n.d.). Retrieved July 9, 2022, from https://code
.visualstudio.com/docs/editor/intellisense

Java in Visual Studio Code. (n.d.). Retrieved July 9, 2022, from https://code.visu-
alstudio.com/docs/languages/java

JavaScript Programming with Visual Studio Code. (n.d.). Retrieved July 9, 2022,
from https://code.visualstudio.com/docs/languages/javascript

JSON Editing in Visual Studio Code. (n.d.). Retrieved July 9, 2022, from https://
code.visualstudio.com/docs/languages/json

Jupyter. (n.d.). Visual Studio Marketplace. Retrieved July 9, 2022, from https://marketplace.visualstudio.com/items?itemName=ms-toolsai.jupyter

Linting Python in Visual Studio Code. (n.d.). Retrieved July 9, 2022, from https://code.visualstudio.com/docs/python/linting#:~:text=Run%20linting%23, when%20you%20save%20a%20file

Live Sass Compiler. (2001, February 1). Visual Studio Marketplace. https://marketplace.visualstudio.com/items?itemName=ritwickdey.live-sass

Material Theme. (2001, March 1). Visual Studio Marketplace. https://marketplace.visualstudio.com/items?itemName=Equinusocio.vsc-material-theme

Mikejo5000. (2022, April 30). *First Look at the Debugger - Visual Studio (Windows).* https://docs.microsoft.com/en-us/visualstudio/debugger/debugger-feature-tour?view=vs-2022

One Dark Pro. (2001, March 1). Visual Studio Marketplace. https://marketplace.visualstudio.com/items?itemName=zhuangtongfa.Material-theme

PowerShell Editing with Visual Studio Code. (n.d.). Retrieved July 9, 2022, from https://code.visualstudio.com/docs/languages/powershell

Prettier – Code Formatter. (2001, March 1). Visual Studio Marketplace. https://marketplace.visualstudio.com/items?itemName=esbenp.prettier-vscode

Python in Visual Studio Code. (n.d.). Retrieved July 9, 2022, from https://code.visualstudio.com/docs/languages/python

Quokka.js. (2001, March 1). Visual Studio Marketplace. https://marketplace.visualstudio.com/items?itemName=WallabyJs.quokka-vscode

React Native Tools. (2001, May 1). Visual Studio Marketplace. https://marketplace.visualstudio.com/items?itemName=msjsdiag.vscode-react-native

Setting up Visual Studio Code. (n.d.). Retrieved July 9, 2022, from https://code.visualstudio.com/docs/setup/setup-overview

Software Testing Help. (2022, June 29). https://www.softwaretestinghelp.com/visual-studio-code-vs-atom/?nowprocket=1

Sublime Text Keymap and Settings Importer. (2001, March 1). Visual Studio Marketplace. https://marketplace.visualstudio.com/items?itemName=ms-vscode.sublime-keybindings

Tabnine AI Autocomplete for Javascript, Python, Typescript, PHP, Go, Java, Ruby & more. (2001, July 1). Visual Studio Marketplace. https://marketplace.visualstudio.com/items?itemName=TabNine.tabnine-vscode

Team, T. (2022, March 10). *Visual Studio vs. Visual Studio Code.* The Official Tabnine Blog. https://www.tabnine.com/blog/visual-studio-vs-visual-studio-code/?utm_source=rss&utm_medium=rss&utm_campaign=visual-studio-vs-visual-studio-code#:~:text=Before%20getting%20deeper%20into%20the,choose%20one%20over%20the%20other

Terminal. (2001, April 1). Visual Studio Marketplace. https://marketplace.visualstudio.com/items?itemName=formulahendry.terminal

Trott, T. (2019, February 1). *Visual Studio Code - Can it Beat Notepad++?* Retrieved September 19, 2022, from https://lonewolfonline.net/vs-code-vs-notepad/

TypeScript Programming with Visual Studio Code. (n.d.). Retrieved July 9, 2022, from https://code.visualstudio.com/docs/languages/typescript

Version Control in Visual Studio Code. (n.d.). Retrieved July 9, 2022, from https://code.visualstudio.com/docs/editor/versioncontrol

Visual Studio. (n.d.). *Visual Studio Marketplace.* Extensions for Visual Studio Family of Products. Retrieved July 9, 2022, from https://marketplace.visualstudio.com/vscode

Visual Studio 2022 Community Edition – Download Latest Free Version. (2021, December 20). https://visualstudio.microsoft.com/vs/community/#:~:text=09%2D08%3A00-,Visual%20Studio%20Community,web%20applications%20and%20cloud%20services

Visual Studio Code. (2015, April 29). Wikipedia. https://en.wikipedia.org/wiki/Visual_Studio_Code#:~:text=Visual%20Studio%20Code%20was%20first,and%20made%20available%20on%20GitHub. Last edited September 8, 2022.

The Visual Studio Code Command-line Options. (n.d.). Retrieved July 9, 2022, from https://code.visualstudio.com/docs/editor/command-line

Visual Studio Code Key Bindings. (n.d.). Retrieved July 9, 2022, from https://code.visualstudio.com/docs/getstarted/keybindings

Visual Studio Code Tips and Tricks. (n.d.). Retrieved July 9, 2022, from https://code.visualstudio.com/docs/getstarted/tips-and-tricks

Visual Studio Code User Interface. (n.d.). Retrieved July 9, 2022, from https://code.visualstudio.com/docs/getstarted/userinterface#:~:text=At%20its%20heart%2C%20Visual%20Studio,the%20files%20you%20have%20opened

Visual Studio Code Vs Atom: Which Code Editor is Better. (2022, June 29). Software Testing Help. https://www.softwaretestinghelp.com/visual-studio-code-vs-atom/#:~:text=Visual%20Studio%20Code%20has%20a%20greater%20number%20of%20built%2Din,easy%20to%20add%20and%20configure

What is IDE or Integrated Development Environments?. (n.d.). Veracode. Retrieved July 9, 2022, from https://www.veracode.com/security/integrated-development-environment#:~:text=Languages%20That%20Are%20Supported%20by%20IDE&text=However%2C%20multiple%2Dlanguage%20IDEs%2C,C%2B%2B%20and%20more)%20do%20exist

What is the Purpose of Text Editors? (n.d.). Quora. Retrieved July 9, 2022, from https://www.quora.com/What-is-the-purpose-of-text-editors

What is the Rich Text Editor? (n.d.). Retrieved July 9, 2022, from https://weblearn.ox.ac.uk/portal/help/TOCDisplay/content.hlp?docId=whatistherichtexteditor

Working with GitHub in Visual Studio Code. (n.d.). Retrieved July 9, 2022, from https://code.visualstudio.com/docs/editor/github

Index

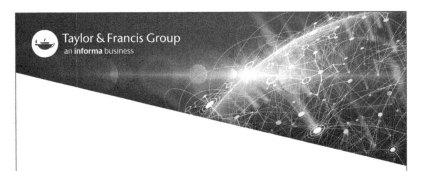

Printed in the United States
by Baker & Taylor Publisher Services